The Gospel of Mark

The Gospel of Mark

An Author's Creation

Pete Sinclair

RESOURCE *Publications* • Eugene, Oregon

THE GOSPEL OF MARK
An Author's Creation

Resource Publications
An Imprint of Wipf and Stock Publishers
199 W. 8th Ave., Suite 3
Eugene, OR 97401

www.wipfandstock.com

PAPERBACK ISBN: 979-8-3852-7865-7
HARDCOVER ISBN: 979-8-3852-7866-4
EBOOK ISBN: 979-8-3852-7867-1

VERSION NUMBER 04/06/26

Contents

Author's Note

THIS MANUSCRIPT HAS NOT been edited by a third-party copyeditor. I am not an academic, and I have written in the only voice I know—a plain, koine-English style that reflects the spirit of the work.

Introduction

Regardless of our denomination, most of us inherit a set of beliefs we are expected to affirm. These often include the conviction that the scriptures must be read literally because they are the word of God, that they contain no contradictions, that Jesus is one with the Father and the Holy Spirit, that Mary was a virgin, and, in some traditions that she is the mother of God.

This pattern began with Paul and continued through second-generation leaders such as Ignatius of Antioch, who urged unity through shared doctrine. That unity became formalized some seventeen hundred years ago at the Council of Nicaea, when church leaders gathered to determine what Christians were required to believe. Paul's call for unity may have provided the premise for this effort, as there was not unanimity among the churches. However, the Arians believed that Jesus was fully human and not one in substance with the Father and the Holy Spirit, and were excommunicated at the council for holding that view.

What I have found in my study is that prescribed beliefs handed down by church leadership can create a diversion that interferes with how the scriptures speak to us. We read more faithfully when we set the church's expectations aside and listen to the text for ourselves with open eyes and a willingness to ask questions.

Can we read the scriptures through a lens other than the one we've inherited? It is not easy, not only because of long-standing doctrines and the communities that uphold them, but because we are to believe that the Bible is Holy Spirit inspired. Yet through my studies I have found that the four Gospels and Paul's authentic letters do not always agree with one another. Are we willing to notice the differences? And what do we do if our reading leads us to an understanding that differs from what our tradition has taught us? If that happens, am I then no longer Christian, like the Arians?

My study of the Gospel of Mark is an attempt to recover what the author's message may have been for the churches he addressed. What follows does not move through the Gospel in a literal sequence from chapter one to the end. Instead, I begin with what first drew my attention and proceed in the order in which the different groups of insights emerged.

What if the Gospel of Mark is not a factual account of Jesus' life, but a literary creation presenting itself as historical reality? In exploring this question, I have come to see the Gospel as more than a narrative. It is a work crafted to convey the vision of an author who centered his message on inclusivity and the potential of a community built on care and compassion for the other person. Through the actions of his Jesus, the author challenges us to imagine what becomes possible when societal barriers fall and the needs of the many are met through the selfless acts of others. His creative storytelling invites us back to the purpose of faith and the possibilities of the Christian community.

In the fall of 1993, I began a research project intended to prove that my Christian theology was not "all wet," as a fellow church member suggested, nor simply the product of my liberal social philosophy. I believed then, and still do, that my social life and politics are shaped by my understanding of the Christian scriptures, not the other way around. It has struck me that many who read the Gospels do so to reassure themselves of what they have been led to believe in their religion. My study changed my understanding of the Gospels and Paul's authentic letters, and how they shape the way I approach my Christian faith.

When I began, I knew I had to confront the challenge of studying the scripture objectively, weighing the current understanding of the Gospel against whatever I found. I resolved to focus solely on the author's words, making a deliberate effort to set aside previous influences from denominational doctrines, sermons, commentaries, and religion classes. To do this, I chose to study one book of the Bible in depth, allowing it to speak to me, as it were. I relied on the Revised Standard Version and aimed to remain open to whatever conclusions arose, whether or not they aligned with my prior beliefs. I selected a book from the Christian scriptures and decided it would be one of the Gospels, believing that a Gospel would take me back to the historical Jesus as closely as possible. Ultimately, I chose Mark, widely regarded as the earliest Gospel and, being the shortest of the four, a manageable starting point.

At the time, I had a fairly sophisticated library that included the original and revised Bible Commentary sets, books written by participants in the Jesus Seminar, and many others. Yet I refused to use any of them, not wanting outside sources to shape my conclusions; ironically, those sources would not have helped me with what I eventually discovered. I also knew I would be studying an English translation rather than the Greek in which the Christian scriptures were originally written. Even so, I eventually brought out my Greek New Testament, the Liddell and Scott Greek–English lexicon, and Strong's Bible Concordance to assist my study.

Through my many years of study, I found that the author of Mark used an outline in at least one place and employed what others call the bookends and insertion technique in several others. These features show that Mark is not a simple historical account but a carefully crafted work. I also discovered that the author used what I call wordplay, which helped me understand why Jesus would curse a fig tree, why he called James and John the sons of thunder, the location of Dalmanutha, and the identities of Barabbas and Bartholomew.

I came to see that the author drew on previously written material: *Prometheus Bound* by Aeschylus, the *Aeneid* by Virgil, and Paul's letters to the Corinthians, Galatians, and Romans. I now believe that Mark was likely written to be used for a baptismal ritual and that it is more closely related to Greek culture than to what is typically called the Judeo–Christian tradition. Finally, I think I have uncovered the name, or at least the pseudonym, of the author.

The term Judeo–Christian was originally used to describe Jews who converted to Christianity. Today, however, many use the term to link the older religion with the newer one, often without knowing its original meaning. A common example is the periodic call to display the Ten Commandments, a distinctly Judean text, on government property. This impulse seems rooted in the assumption that the Christian scriptures stand in direct continuity with the Hebrew scriptures. Interestingly, I have never heard anyone call for displaying the commandments of Jesus: to love God with all that one is, and to love one's neighbor as oneself.

I find the persistent effort to display the Ten Commandments especially interesting in light of Paul's words: "For freedom Christ has set us free; stand fast therefore, and do not submit again to a yoke of slavery. Now I, Paul, say to you that if you receive circumcision, Christ will be of no benefit to you. I testify again to every man who receives circumcision that he is bound to keep the whole law. You are severed from Christ, you who would be justified by the law; you have fallen away from grace" (Gal 5:1–4).

One of the arguments that distinguishes my findings from what is often assumed is that the author of Mark did not simply send a written document to the churches established by Paul, but relied on a rhapsode to deliver it. A rhapsode was a performer who recited from memory or from a written text—anything from Homer and Herodotus to the news of the day, and quite possibly a gospel. In one of Plato's dialogues, he portrays Ion, a rhapsode, as either an interpreter who honors his God-given gift or someone who exploits it for monetary gain. Because of the wordplay I found in Mark, I believe the gospel was first transmitted orally to its earliest hearers.

The gospel contains homonyms and other linguistic nuances that would have been conveyed most effectively through an oral performance. A member of one of Paul's churches reading from a scroll or papyrus would not have been able to communicate these subtleties to the listeners. In fact, we face a similar limitation today: reading the gospel in English leaves us without the nuances a rhapsode could express through the Greek language.

Through this study I explored material I otherwise might never have considered: Greek and Roman myth, ancient Greek history and culture, the Greek language, tragedies such as *Prometheus Bound* and the *Agamemnon*, and literature like the *Iliad* and the *Aeneid*. I was also introduced to people such as Socrates, Plato, Pythagoras, Zeno, Sappho, and Herodotus. I did not consult commentaries on Mark, but I did take seriously insights shared in friendly conversations, including the bookends-and-insertion theory and the possibility that Mark was used for a baptismal ritual.

I also read H. D. F. Kitto's *Greek Tragedy*, James M. Robinson's introduction to *The Nag Hammadi Scriptures*, and Joseph McCabe's *Myth of the Resurrection*, all of which I recommend to anyone interested in exploring the roots of the Christian tradition. I read many more books than I can now recall, most of which I have since given away or misplaced, leaving memory as my primary tool. When I began, I did not imagine this study would become something I might want to publish, and I did not keep the books for reference. Much of what I cite comes from memory, supported by occasional confirmation through Google AI and Microsoft Copilot.

The Gospel of Mark was written by someone who knew far more than the basic stories about Jesus. The author was familiar with Greek tragedy, Roman literature, and the Hebrew scriptures, and he shaped the gospel with the kind of skill that comes from education and time spent with texts. Mark isn't the work of a simple storyteller passing along memories; it reflects a mind that understood how literature, performance, and symbol could work together.

The way the Gospel uses Greek wordplay, classical themes, and ritual imagery points to someone who lived in a Greek world and knew how stories were performed and heard. He could draw from myth, scripture, and the politics of his day and weave them into a single narrative without losing the thread. That kind of synthesis doesn't come from an untrained follower. It comes from someone who approached the Gospel as a crafted work meant to be listened to, interpreted, and carried into the life of a community.

This kind of author fits well within the world of the early Pauline churches, where education, rhetoric, and theological imagination often came together. Even if we cannot name him with certainty, the Gospel itself shows us the kind of person he was: educated, thoughtful, creative, and deeply engaged with the cultural world around him. Seeing the author this way helps us read Mark not as a simple record of events, but as a deliberate and meaningful creation shaped for its first hearers.

1

The Outline and the Use of Wordplay

I REMEMBER THE FIRST day I opened my Bible to the Gospel of Mark. I began at chapter 1, verse 1, and everything I read was the same as it had always been; nothing caught my eye; until I reached the courtyard scene.

I realized that if the courtyard scene were removed, the narrative would move directly from Pilate's interrogation of Jesus to his being led away to be scourged and crucified, which is likely the actual sequence of events. But that is not what Mark wrote. Seeing this forced me to confront a question: what in this narrative reflects history, and what reflects the author's creative work? Was he weaving fragments of what actually happened into a literary design rather than recording a historical event?

While considering the impact of the courtyard scene, I reread the entire passion narrative and discovered that the author had arranged it according to a deliberate outline. A rhapsode would have memorized this structure, making it easier to recite the gospel as the author intended. It begins with Judas's betrayal and Jesus' prayer in Gethsemane and concludes with Jesus' final cry and the centurion's declaration.

THE OUTLINE

a. Judas betrays Jesus (14:10–11)

b. Jesus prays: "Abba, Father, take this cup from me; yet not my will but yours be done" (14:38)

c. Jesus is taken to the high priest (14:53)

d. Jesus is tried before Caiaphas: "Are you the Christ, the Son of the Blessed?" He answers yes (14:61–62)

e. The priests condemn him, spit on him, and strike him (14:64–65)

a. Peter betrays Jesus by denying he knows him (14:66–72)

c. Jesus is taken to Pilate (15:1b)

d. Jesus is interrogated by Pilate: "Are you the king of the Jews?" He answers, "You say it" (15:2b)

e. Pilate sends Jesus to be scourged; the soldiers braid a crown of thorns, strike him, and spit upon him (15:15–20)

b. Jesus prays as he dies: "My God, my God, why have you forsaken me?" (15:34b)

d. The centurion identifies him: "Truly this man was the Son of God!" (15:39b)

Though not perfect, this outline—with its duplications within the passion—revealed to me that Mark's account was, at least in part, the author's creation. It also prepared me to examine its three central components: the interrogations by the priests and Pilate; the actors in the courtyard scene—Pilate, the King of the Jews, the priests, and the crowd; and finally, the inclusion of Barabbas.

THE INTERROGATIONS

The priests ask Jesus, "Are you the Christ, the Son of the Blessed?" Jesus replies, "I am; and you will see the Son of Man seated at the right hand of Power and coming with the clouds of heaven"

(14:61b–62). Notably, Mark, Matthew, and Luke do not record Jesus predicting the destruction of the temple during this questioning.

Then Jesus is brought before Pilate: "As soon as it was morning the chief priests, with the elders and scribes and the whole council, held a consultation; and they bound Jesus and led him away and delivered him to Pilate." Pilate asks him, "Are you the King of the Jews?" Jesus answers, "You say it." The chief priests accused him of many things, and Pilate presses him again: "Have you no answer to make? See how many charges they bring against you." But Jesus remains silent, and Pilate wonders (15:1–5).

This raises an obvious question: who was present to record these exchanges? How did Mark know what Jesus said to the priests or to Pilate? The narrative gives no indication that any of Jesus' followers were present, which suggests that these scenes reflect the author's theological and literary aims rather than eyewitness reporting.

The questioning by the priests differs sharply from that of Pilate. The priests ask a religious question: "Are you the Christ, the Son of the Blessed?" Pilate asks a political one: "Are you the King of the Jews?" These are not interchangeable. They carry different meanings for the questioners, and Jesus' responses differ accordingly. The priests react with outrage to Jesus' claim to be the Son of God. Pilate, however, would have had little interest in the religious beliefs of the locals; his concern was whether Jesus posed a threat to Roman authority.

Jesus' answer to Pilate, "You say it," appears ambiguous and many claim that the response was "that is your claim against me." The meaning will become clearer when we consider Pilate's role as prefect. He was Caesar's representative and functioned as the proxy ruler of Judea. In that sense, he was the one who really was king of the Jews. Jesus' reply can therefore be understood as: You are the one saying this—for yourself.

Herod the Great had been appointed king of the Jews by the Romans in 40 BCE. His son, Herod Antipas, ruled at the time Jesus was on trial, but only as a tetrarch with limited authority over a small region of Judea; the Romans never granted him the title king of the Jews.

ACTORS IN THE COURTYARD

After Jesus is led away from Pilate, his name does not appear again until he is taken to be scourged.

Throughout the gospel, the crowd follows Jesus. Yet in the courtyard they condemn the King of the Jews and demand the release of Barabbas instead. This striking reversal raises a question: why would the crowd suddenly want the King of the Jews executed if that figure is Jesus? Are we expected to accept that Jesus is the King of the Jews because of Pilate's question? I argue no, because within the political world of the narrative, Pilate is the one who functions as the King of the Jews.

What, then, does Pilate do with the King of the Jews? In my view, nothing, because he is the king of the Jews—the Roman-appointed authority whom both the chief priests and the crowd resent and fear. The Pilate of history would not have yielded to either group. He would act with impunity, and any attempt to portray him as pressured or reluctant is conjecture, even wishful thinking. Philo of Alexandria (*On the Embassy to Gaius* 153–58) and Josephus (*The Jewish Wars* 3.506 *and Antiquities of the Jews* 2.233–35) record that Pilate was a strict and cruel prefect.

WHO IS BARABBAS?

"Do you want me to release for you the King of the Jews?" For Pilate perceived that it was out of envy that the chief priests had delivered him up. But the chief priests stirred up the crowd to have him release Barabbas instead (15:9–11).

This raises immediate questions: whom do the priests envy, and who is Barabbas that the crowd would prefer him? Why did the priests stir the crowd up to have Pilate release Barabbas?

Mark offers a telling detail: "Among the rebels in prison, who had committed murder in the insurrection, there was a man called Barabbas" (15:7).

In 26 CE, just before Pilate became prefect of Judaea, the previous Roman prefect took funds from the temple treasury to build an aqueduct. The priests objected fiercely, and according to Josephus (*Antiquities* 18.3.2 and 18.60–62), the unrest escalated into a violent insurrection that lasted nearly a decade. It was during this period that Jesus was executed. This background makes it even less likely that Pilate would have deferred to the priests or the crowd in the way the narrative suggests.

BARABBAS AS A LITERARY FIGURE

In chapter 4 of Mark, Jesus teaches in parables and says that some will "see but not perceive" and "hear but not understand." In other words, not everything in Mark should be taken at face value. This raises a natural question: how does Jesus relate to Barabbas?

The consistent presence of Barabbas in all four Gospels led me to wonder whether the later authors understood Mark's use of the name. Mark seems to have employed a deliberate literary device for his name, one carrying a deeper symbolic meaning. As I noted in the introduction, Mark often uses the bookends-and-insertion technique, and he uses it here.

Barabbas appears only in the courtyard scene, which is between two moments in which Jesus is named; first after his interrogation by Pilate, and then when he is led away to be scourged. The use of the bookends are meant to interpret the insertion: the figure named in both bookends is Jesus, and the inserted figure is Barabbas. The question becomes: how does Jesus relate to Barabbas?

To answer this, we return to the beginning of Mark. "The beginning of the gospel of Jesus Christ, the Son of God" (1:1). At Jesus' baptism, a voice from heaven says, "Thou art my beloved Son" (1:11). At the transfiguration, the voice declares, "This is my beloved Son" (9:7). In Gethsemane, Jesus prays, "Abba, Father" (14:36). And before the priests, he affirms that he is the Son of the Blessed (14:61–62). In every case, the relationship is the same: Jesus is the son, and God is the father.

The prayer in the garden brings this relationship to a personal level: Abba, Father. This language points directly to the name Bar-abbas, which can be broken down into bar = son and abbas = father or son of the father. This is the same relationship the gospel uses for Jesus and God in the passages above. Are Jesus and Barabbas one and the same?

BARABBAS AS JESUS' LITERARY DOUBLE

If the Barabbas figure is a literary double of Jesus rather than a historical prisoner, what was the author's intent for those who first heard the gospel? This question becomes sharper when we remember that Mark was written after Paul's final letters.

I have come to see the scene as serving three purposes:

1. Barabbas represents those who pray "Abba, Father," as in Galatians 4:6–7 and Romans 8:15–17, those who are called sons of God and joint heirs with Christ.
2. Jesus is cast in the role of the insurrectionist, the very charge that would lead to his crucifixion.
3. The baptismal candidate, in being chosen, is released when Jesus dies on the cross.

Jesus is taken away to be executed for the many, while Barabbas is released. If Jesus embodies the son of the Father and Barabbas represents that same identity, the contrast becomes symbolic. One is released through baptism; the other is executed. In Mark's symbolic world, Jesus' crucifixion becomes the means by which those who pray "Abba, Father" are released.

Where Did Mark Get Abba?

Who heard Jesus pray to Abba, given that the disciples were asleep (14:37–41)? The most likely explanation is that the author used language familiar to the communities who first heard the gospel, the communities evangelized by Paul (Gal 4:6 and Rom

8:15). And why do the other gospels omit Abba in the garden prayer, even though all of them include Barabbas?

This suggests that the author may have belonged to Paul's circle, perhaps as a convert or someone shaped by the same theological currents.

WHY DID JESUS CURSE A FIG TREE?

The cursed and withered fig tree (the bookends) and the temple cleansing (the insertion) never made much sense to me. Why would Jesus curse something not bound by ethics, morals, or the Torah? A fig tree cannot influence anyone; it can only satisfy hunger or offer shade. And why expect fruit when it was not the season for them? I began to suspect that the author was using a play on words that would have made immediate sense to his audience. Since I had already used the bookends-and-insertion structure elsewhere, I wondered whether it might help explain this scene as well.

The First Bookend

"On the following day, when they came from Bethany, he was hungry. And seeing in the distance a fig tree in leaf, he went to see if he could find anything on it. When he came to it, he found nothing but leaves, for it was not the season for figs. And he said to it, 'May no one ever eat fruit from you again.' And his disciples heard it" (11:12–14).

The Insertion

"And they came to Jerusalem. And he entered the temple and began to drive out those who sold and those who bought in the temple, and he overturned the tables of the moneychangers and the seats of those who sold pigeons; and he would not allow anyone to carry anything through the temple. And he taught, saying,

'Is it not written, My house shall be called a house of prayer for all nations? But you have made it a den of robbers'" (11:15–17).

The Greek word translated as "all nations" is *ethnos* (ἔθνος), a term debated among scholars. Some argue it means all humanity; others say it refers specifically to Gentiles. In Greek myth, Hermes is the patron of robbers, commerce, and wealth, a symbolic image that Greek converts would have recognized immediately. The accusation of a "den of robbers" would have carried cultural resonance for them.

The Second Bookend

"As they passed by in the morning, they saw the fig tree withered away to its roots. And Peter remembered and said to him, 'Master, look! The fig tree which you cursed has withered.' And Jesus answered them, 'Have faith in God. . . therefore I tell you, whatever you ask in prayer, believe that you have received it, and it will be yours'" (11:20–22, 24).

When I consulted the Greek New Testament and lexicon, I found that the word for fig tree is *sukē* (συκῆ). At first it meant nothing to me, until I noticed a homonym: *psuchē* (ψυχή), the word from which we get "psyche," meaning soul, life, or self in ancient Greek. That discovery convinced me that the gospel was likely performed by a rhapsode, not simply read aloud by a member of the congregation. A rhapsode would have emphasized the sound of the words, allowing the homonym to land with force.

My Interpretation

In the first bookend, Jesus and his disciples encounter a soul (a *sukē/psuchē*) that is barren, fruitless, stale, and out of season. In the insertion, Jesus confronts unnamed figures who have turned the house of prayer into a den of robbers. In the second bookend, the fig tree (or barren soul) has withered to its roots.

The parallel becomes clear: the withered fig tree represents the rulers of the temple, whose spiritual lives have dried up. They are fruitless, lifeless, and corrupt. In contrast, the disciples are encouraged to have faith, to pray, and to trust that God will respond. There will be no commandments to obey. No priests to mediate. No temple required. Forgiveness and life come from the Father through the Spirit, not through the temple system.

This, in my view, is the second strong example of Mark's wordplay. My interpretation may be only that—an interpretation—but it makes far more sense to me than many explanations I have read for why Jesus would curse a fig tree that was out of season.

THE SONS OF THUNDER

Many scholars have noted that the author of Mark holds a dim view of James, John, and Peter. Like Peter, who rebukes Jesus, misunderstands the parables, and ultimately denies him, and James and John reveal the same inability to perceive what Jesus is actually doing.

One common interpretation of Jesus calling them the "sons of thunder" is that their preaching style was loud, fiery, and thunderous. I have never found that convincing. Are we to imagine the first-century disciples preaching like Billy Sunday did in the early twentieth century? Oratory in the first century was measured, rational, rhythmic, perhaps metered, but not the firebrand exhortation of modern revivalists.

For a long time, I struggled with this wordplay because I was focusing on the wrong word. I kept trying to make sense of *Boanerges* (Βοανηργές), which Mark interprets as "sons of thunder" (3:17). But the key was not in the nickname—it was in the father's name.

The father of James and John is Zebedee, or rather, in the Greek text, *Zebedaiou* (Ζεβεδαίου). As the father of these two disciples, his name carries symbolic weight, much like "God" and "Abba" function as names for the father of Jesus. And since the author of Mark seems to stand within Paul's theological orbit, it is worth remembering that James and John consistently opposed Paul over his lack of commitment to the law. It should not surprise us that the author might use pointed language to describe the sons of *Zebedaiou*.

When I looked more closely at the Greek, the first part of the name—Ze—did not yield much. But the second part, *bedaiou*, did. It has a homonym of sorts: *bdeō* (βδέω). Placing them side by side—*Zebedaiou* and *Ze-bdeō*—did not reveal much at first, until I considered the definition: it means "to break wind." Breaking wind can be thunderous, and certainly repulsive.

It may sound sacrilegious or provocative, especially since it appears in the Holy Bible, but it makes good sense to me. The author may have used this homonym intentionally to discredit the two disciples. A rhapsode performing the gospel could easily emphasize the sound of the name, *Ze-bdeō*, in a way that would make the audience grasp the pun far more clearly than a church member reading *Zebedaiou*, or any of us encountering only the English name Zebedee. The theology of James and John, the sons of Ze-breaking-wind, stands in sharp contrast to the theology of Jesus and Paul, the sons of Abba.

THE LOCATION OF DALMANUTHA

The author of Mark has puzzled Christian scholars and skeptics alike with this line: "And he sent them away; and immediately he got into the boat with his disciples and went to the district of Dalmanutha" (8:10). Most attempts to locate Dalmanutha have focused on the western shore of the Sea of Galilee near Magdala because of Matthew 15:39, where he replaces the name with Magadan. Still, archaeologists have found nothing in the area using either name.

One reason for this confusion is the assumption that Dalmanutha must be a town. But the English text says "district," and the Greek word is *dēmos* (δῆμος), meaning an area or part of a larger whole. There has never been a district called Dalmanutha anywhere near Magdala, or anywhere in Israel. That alone should have halted the search in Galilee. Yet the question persists, especially among Mythists who argue that Jesus never existed and use the "non-existence" of Dalmanutha as evidence. The problem is not that Dalmanutha doesn't exist; it's that scholars have been looking in the wrong place.

The earlier enigmas—Bar/abbas, *sukē/psuchē*, and *Zebedaiou/Ze-bdeō*—relied on homonyms and wordplay. Dalmanutha is different. I searched every possible angle in my abridged lexicon and found nothing. Eventually I went to the Louisville Presbyterian Theological Seminary library to consult its unabridged Liddell and Scott lexicon.

It is important to remember that the gospel was recited from memory or from a scroll, so a strict Greek-to-English translation will not always capture the clues a rhapsode would emphasize. I could not make sense of Dalmanutha until I checked the Greek spelling in the New Testament. Like Zebedee, the English form obscures the Greek. The word is *Dalmanoutha* (Δαλμανουθα). Using the lexicon, I broke the word down:

Once the spelling is correct, the components fall into place:

- *Dalm* (Δαλμ)—a man from Dalmatia
- *an* (ἀν)—like our word *sans*, meaning "without"
- *outha* (οὐθα)—"surely not"

Dalm-an-outha: "The Dalmatian would surely not be without."

Without what? The gospel.

Dalmatia is nowhere near Israel or the Sea of Galilee. It lies across the Adriatic Sea from Rome, north of modern-day Greece. And Dalmatia was a district—a part of the whole—of ancient Illyricum, which is likely the last place Paul worked before traveling to Rome and his execution.

Dalm was used informally to refer to someone from Dalmatia. It is not surprising that Greek biblical scholars overlooked this; most were working within the long-held assumption that Jesus never left Israel, an assumption that naturally limited where they were willing to look.

Dalmatia's connection to Paul appears in Romans 15:19, where he thanks God that "from Jerusalem and as far around as

Illyricum I have fully preached the gospel of Christ." Illyricum and *Dalmanoutha* are each mentioned only once in the Bible, and the two references are related. Mark certainly drew on Paul's reference.

Why do Matthew, Luke, and John omit *Dalmanoutha*? Perhaps because they understood exactly what Mark meant and chose not to repeat it. Did they recognize that Mark was referencing Paul's work outside Judea rather than an episode in Jesus' life?

This wordplay led me to consider that the church in the district of Dalmatia may have been the first community to hear the Gospel of Mark performed. They would have immediately recognized the reference to their homeland. I also believe this may have been where Paul wrote his letter to the Romans. His use of Abba in that letter was probably part of his evangelic message to the Dalmatians.

A few scholars have proposed interpretations that brush up against mine. Some have argued that Dalmanutha is not a Galilean location at all and may carry Roman or Illyrian resonance, and one interpretation even links the name to a Roman military formation.

THE IDENTITY OF BARTHOLOMEW

Mark's list of the twelve includes Bartholomew, whose identity is less clear than the others. If we apply the bookends-and-insertion structure here, a pattern emerges.

Mark's list of the twelve:

Peter
James
John
Andrew
Philip
Bartholomew
Matthew
Thomas
James the son of Alphaeus
Thaddaeus
Simon the Cananaean

Judas

The first bookend

Simon Peter—betrayed Jesus and Paul

The insertion

Bartholomew—son of who?

The second bookend

Judas Iscariot—betrayed Jesus

The bookends are the two betrayers, Simon Peter and Judas. The insertion is Bartholomew. On the surface this may not seem significant, but the Greek opens possibilities. Bartholomew (English) is *Bartholomaion* (Βαρθολομαῖον), meaning "son of Tholomaion," which itself yields little. But *Ptolemaion* (Πτολεμαῖον) is strikingly similar to Tholomaion and refers to the Ptolemaic family from Macedonia. Ptolemy was a general in Alexander the Great's army, and after Alexander's death, the Ptolemies ruled Egypt for nearly three centuries. Macedonia, in the early Christian era, was part of the Greek world, north of what we now call Greece and south of Illyricum and Dalmatia.

Barptolemaion (Βαρ-Πτολεμαῖον) could be understood as son of the Greeks.

This interpretation underscores the tension between Peter's role in Paul's mission and the incorporation of Greek proselytes. The insertion may represent the Greek proselytes Paul brought into the congregation, which relates to Galatians: "When Cephas (Peter) came to Antioch I opposed him to his face, because he stood condemned. . ." (2:11–13). Peter betrayed Paul and his converts (*Bar-ptolemaion*) when he withdrew from the Greeks and aligned himself with the circumcision party after having eaten and socialized with them.

No scholar has proposed the interpretation I outline here. A few have noted Mark's literary use of names or the tension between Peter and Paul, but none apply these insights to Bartholomew or to the structure of the Twelve. No existing scholarship connects Bartholomew to *Bar-ptolomaion*, to Macedonia, or to the incorporation of Greek proselytes. This interpretation is my own.

THE GOSPEL GIVEN BY A RHAPSODE

My hypothesis is that a rhapsode recited the gospel from a scroll or codex until he had mastered it well enough to perform it from memory. He would then have left the document with a member of one of the Pauline churches before departing for the next mission church. Or he may have dictated it to a scribe for safekeeping. In either case, it would have been copied as it aged, and any attempt to preserve it for antiquity would have been impossible in that era.

The chain of people copying the gospel, over eighty to nearly three hundred years, would not have had the instructions the author originally gave the rhapsode. Even if the original document contained the wordplay, those who copied it quite possibly changed the words to make them understandable. My conclusion is that the copy we possess today is not identical to the manuscript used by the rhapsode, assuming he even recited from a document rather than entirely from memory.

Despite these uncertainties, my interpretation explains each of the wordplays far better than anything I have encountered in traditional scholarship.

No scholar has proposed the rhapsodic transmission model I outline here. While some have explored oral performance in early Christianity or noted Mark's use of Greek wordplay, none connect these features to a trained rhapsode, a performance script, or a Pauline transmission chain. This interpretation is my own.

It is important to acknowledge the limits of what can be confirmed about how the Gospel of Mark was first transmitted. These limits include the challenges inherent to biblical studies, the lack of archaeological evidence, and the absence of contemporary documents that could verify the existence of a rhapsode or confirm that this method of delivery was used at the time.

The wordplay I attribute to a rhapsode cannot be verified directly, since oral performance leaves no physical trace. The earliest evidence we possess is a fragment of Mark dated between 150 and 250 CE—almost certainly not the original, but a copy several generations removed.

2

The Author's Use of Previously Written Material

Through my study of Greek history and culture, which included mythology, I came across the story of a Titan crucified by Zeus. This led me to further exploration, where I discovered the tragedy *Prometheus Bound* by Aeschylus. As I looked deeper, I learned that, like Jesus, Prometheus was a son of god who was crucified for saving the human race. This revelation marked a pivotal moment in my journey and set the stage for the next phase of my study.

I eventually discovered that *Prometheus Bound*, Virgil's *Aeneid*, and Paul's first letter to the Corinthians along with Galatians, and Romans were used by the author to construct his gospel.

PROMETHEUS BOUND

Almost three thousand years ago, ancient Greek mythology gave rise to the story of Prometheus, a Titan who helped Zeus overthrow Kronus to become the chief god of Olympus. Prometheus, along with his brother Epimetheus (husband of Pandora), became central figures in myths that shaped understandings of human origins and the trials of life. In one strain of the myth, Prometheus stole fire from Zeus, either after Zeus had taken it from humanity or to offer it as a gift for their survival along with technological advancements for farming and war.

The most relevant version for this manuscript involves Prometheus deceiving Zeus during a sacrificial tribute by withholding the meat and offering only fat and bones inside the carcass. Enraged by this trickery, Zeus ordered Prometheus to be crucified on a stone cliff at the edge of the wilderness, strikingly similar to Jesus' crucifixion outside the city in the wilderness. As punishment, an eagle would devour Prometheus' liver daily, only for it to grow back and then every next day the bird would return for the same meal.

Roughly five hundred years after the formation of the Promethean myths, a festival honoring the god Dionysus in Athens hosted a contest for tragedy trilogies. Aeschylus, often called the father of tragedy, entered his *Prometheia*, a trilogy about Prometheus and his feud with Zeus. The first part, *Prometheus Bound*, begins with Zeus crucifying Prometheus and ends with the Titan's descent into the black depths of Tartarus, what we would call Hell. Unfortunately, the second and third parts of the trilogy (*Prometheus Unbound* and *Prometheus the Fire Starter*?) are largely lost to antiquity, surviving only in fragments. These remnants provide some insight into their content, though scholars can do little beyond speculation.

Why, then, has *Prometheus Bound* endured intact while its sequels did not, despite the high regard for both Aeschylus and his trilogy? It's worth noting that some scholars debate whether the trilogy existed in full or was even authored by Aeschylus. However, the prevailing consensus supports its existence, bolstered by the fragments that suggest a coherent trilogy.

The answer to my question may lie within *Prometheus Bound* itself. Aeschylus adapted the myth of Prometheus to suit his vision and presented it at the festival for judgment. In his narrative, Prometheus is crucified not only for deceiving Zeus with a sham sacrifice but also for saving humanity from destruction. His name, Prometheus, means forethought, which provides further insight.

Prometheus, anticipating the probable suffering he would have to endure, knowingly accepted Zeus' wrath. Jesus, similarly, foresaw his fate: "The Son of man must suffer many things. . .and be killed, and after three days rise again" (Mark 8:31). In *Prometheus Bound*, Hermes prophesies that a god (Heracles) will rescue Prometheus from his torment, effectively resurrecting him—the same as Jesus.

What is the reason for *Prometheus Bound*'s enduring legacy while its counterparts have been lost? I believe it is the Greek's sense of indebtedness to its creator and benefactor, a figure who sacrificed himself for their survival. The audience would resonate with a son of a god standing against the chief deity to secure humanity's future. Christians hold similar sentiments about Jesus of Nazareth, whose story of sacrifice for those who follow has endured for not quite two thousand years.

Please notice that all of the comparisons share a sequence from beginning to end.

How do the sons of the gods compare?

Both are crucified in similar places, one on the outside of the city near the wilderness and the other at the edge of the wilderness. "And they brought him to a place called Golgotha (which means the place of the skull)" (Mark 15:21a). Golgotha lay outside the walls of Jerusalem, and part of the wilderness. Prometheus, likewise, is crucified at the edge of the earth (*Prometheus Bound* lines 1–21), the mythic wilderness beyond the world of humans.

Both have reluctant executioners, Pilate found no fault with him and wanted to release him (Mark 15:6–15). Hephaestus, a fellow Titan, did not want to take part in the punishment but was commanded by Zeus, so he did what he was told to do (*Prometheus Bound* lines 12–19).

Both have people at the scene who make similar derisive comments, "Aha! You who would destroy the temple and build it in three days, save yourself, and come down from the cross" (Mark 15:29b–30). Strength (Kratos) chastises Prometheus to try and get out of the predicament that he and Hephaestus had put him in (*Prometheus Bound* lines 82–85).

Both have women at their crucifixions, "There were also women looking from afar, among whom were Mary Magdalene, and Mary the mother of James the younger and of Joses, and Salome" (Mark 15:40). The Chorus at the scene is made up of women who enter the tragedy (*Prometheus Bound* lines 126–27).

Both have their respective god's messengers at the scenes, "So also the chief priests mocked him to one another with the scribes, saying, 'he saved others; he cannot save himself" (Mark 15:31). Hermes, the messenger of Zeus, oversaw the execution, enters (*Prometheus Bound* after line 942).

Both have women run away afraid at the end, "And they went out and fled from the tomb; for trembling and astonishment had come upon them; and they said nothing to anyone, for they were afraid" (Mark 16:8). After Prometheus descends into Tartarus and the earth quakes, the Chorus flees (*Prometheus Bound* after line 1093).

While I suppose that each of the above similarities could be coincidental or even that Jesus orchestrated the whole of his events to mirror the myth, I don't think so. What I believe is that the Jesus of the gospels is not the Jesus of history and was never intended to be that person. The authors of the Gospels and in particular Mark had something else in mind. In Mark's case Jesus was a person to fit a personal theology built around the experiences and understanding of what Paul preached (or what Paul was taught by someone while trying to evangelize the people of Greece).

Mark is not the only author of the Christian scriptures who draws on *Prometheus Bound.*

Matthew includes something that Mark does not, "the rocks were split" (27:51). (*Prometheus Bound* line 1077).

Luke (23:44, 45) includes, "It was about the sixth hour, and there was darkness over the whole land until the ninth hour, while the sun failed." (*Prometheus Bound* 1076–1081).

Acts of the Apostles leans on *Prometheus Bound* at the trial of Paul before Agrippa where he has Paul say that the voice from heaven asked him why he kicks at the goads (26:13), the identical language is used by Oceanus to Prometheus (*Prometheus Bound* line 326).

Agrippa tells Paul that he is mad, that his great learning has made him insane (26:24) and Oceanus accuses Prometheus similarly but instead of his learning he accuses him of being more intelligent than the way he is acting (*Prometheus Bound* line 329).

1 Peter writes that Jesus will descend into Hell to free the prisoners, "being put to death in the flesh but made alive in the spirit; in which he went and preached to the spirits in prison" (3:18b-19a). Hermes advised Prometheus that someone would descend into black Tartarus to free him (*Prometheus Bound* line 1026).

The Apostles' Creed uses the 1 Peter quote as part of its language, "He suffered under Pontius Pilate, was crucified, died, and was buried; he descended to hell . . ."—a stunning claim.

The above similarities tell me that other authors of the Christian scriptures knew Mark's resources as well.

AENEID

A little more than two thousand seven hundred years ago, a poet known as Homer wrote the *Iliad*, an epic about the destruction of Troy by the Greeks. Some scholars argue that he may not have been the sole author, or that multiple poets contributed to the work. Among his characters is a brave hero named Aeneas, though he plays only a minor role in the *Iliad* itself.

My search leading to the *Aeneid* began with the idea that Jesus riding into Jerusalem on the back of a young horse might have a relationship to the Greeks entering Troy inside a wooden horse. This connection was partly inspired by Mark 13, where Jesus tells his disciples to observe the buildings of Jerusalem, predicting that one day not one stone would be left upon another.

Since Josephus wrote that the temple was destroyed by fire (*Wars of the Jews* 6.249—6.266), we should consider why Mark describes its destruction as the dismantling of stones. Another problem is the accusation in Mark 14:58 that Jesus intended to destroy the temple made with hands and rebuild one not made with hands. Mark's description of the temple's destruction is closer to the destruction of Priam's temple in the *Aeneid.*

Approximately seven hundred years after the *Iliad* was written, a Roman poet named Virgil composed the *Aeneid,* which follows the hero Aeneas from his escape at Troy to Carthage and then to the land we now call Italy, where he founded Lavinium and laid the foundation for the Roman Empire.

After Venus helped Aeneas escape from Troy, she led him into the Mediterranean Sea with the intent that he would found Rome. But not all the gods were supportive. The goddess Juno (Greek Hera) did everything she could to prevent Aeneas from fulfilling his fate. She induced the Roman god Aeolus (Greek Aiolos) to create a storm that would wreck his ships.

As with *Prometheus Bound,* the parallels between Mark and the Aeneid follow the same narrative sequence from beginning to end, with only two exceptions.

The similarities between Mark and the *Aeneid*

Both are compelled by the gods to their fates: "The Spirit immediately drove him out into the wilderness" (Mark 1:12). Aeneas was driven by the gods to found the land that would become Rome (*Aeneid* Book I lines 15–18).

The storms stilled by Jesus and Neptune: Jesus rebukes the wind and calms the sea (Mark 4:35–41). Aeolus creates a storm that wrecks Aeneas' fleet; Neptune becomes angered and calms the sea (*Aeneid* Book I lines 193–99).

Jesus and Neptune traverse on top of the water: Jesus walks on the sea toward the disciples (Mark 6:47–48). After Neptune calms the sea, he walks across it and enters his chariot (*Aeneid* Book I lines 199–200).

The transfiguration of Jesus and Aeneas: Jesus is transfigured on the mountain, his garments glistening white (Mark 9:2–3). A cloud provided by Venus envelops Aeneas and his captain as they enter Carthage; when it dissipates, Aeneas appears in brilliant white as a god (*Aeneid* Book I lines 563–66; 799–801).

Entrance into the city; Jesus on a horse and the Greeks in a horse. Jesus rides into Jerusalem on a colt (Mark 11:1–7). The

Greeks enter Troy inside a wooden horse, ostensibly a peace offering (*Aeneid* Book II lines 21–29; 264–65).

Items placed before the horses: Followers of Jesus lay garments on the road in front of Jesus (Mark 11:8a). Trojans place rollers beneath the wooden horse to move it into the city (*Aeneid* Book II lines 314–16).

Leafy branches and greenery: "Others spread leafy branches which they had cut from the fields" (Mark 11:8b). Trojans decorate the city with greenery (*Aeneid* Book II lines 333–35).

Hymns are sung: "Hosanna! Blessed is he who comes in the name of the Lord!" (Mark 11:9–10). The young Trojans sing hymns (*Aeneid* Book II lines 319–20).

Destruction of both temples—no stone left on another: "There will not be left here one stone upon another. . ." (Mark 13:2). Defenders atop Priam's temple hurl stones down on the Greeks (*Aeneid* Book II lines 584–87).

Take heed that no one leads you astray—beware of the Greeks: "Take heed that no one leads you astray" (Mark 13:5). A Greek soldier deceives the Trojans into bringing the horse inside the city (*Aeneid* Book II lines 91–93; 206–7).

Nation will rise against nation: "For nation will arise against nation. . ." (Mark 13:8).

Book II of the *Aeneid* recounts the war between Greeks and Trojans.

Flee to the mountains: "Let those who are in Judea flee to the mountains. . ." (Mark 13:14). Aeneas attempts to flee the hopeless battle, carrying Anchises toward the mountains (*Aeneid* Book II line 830).

Those on housetops should not go down: "Let him who is on the housetop not go down. . ." (Mark 13:15). Aeneas awakens, climbs to his roof to see the battle, then descends to fight (*Aeneid* Book II line 600).

Women and their tribulation: "And alas for those who are with child and for those who give suck in those days!" (Mark 13:17). During the fall of Troy, the women huddle together in terror as the battle rages (*Aeneid* Book II lines 632–37).

Only the elect will survive: "If the Lord had not shortened the days. . . the elect. . . would be saved" (Mark 13:20). Aeneas survives—Book II of the *Aeneid* recounts Aeneas' own account of Troy's destruction, and the epic as a whole tells the story of his escape from the carnage, aided by his divine mother, to become the chosen one who would found Rome.

Taken together, these parallels show that the author of Mark drew directly from Virgil's *Aeneid*. The epic was one of the most widely known works in the Roman world at that time, and members of Paul's churches would have recognized the imagery and narrative patterns immediately. The world of Virgil shaped the imagination of the Roman Empire, and it is no surprise that its imagery echoes through the story Mark chose to tell.

The parallels between Mark and the *Aeneid* presented here are the result of my own independent study. While scholars such as Floyd E. Schneider (*Mark Challenges the Aeneid*, 2019) have explored connections between these texts, the specific sequence of parallels and the comparative framework developed in this manuscript are my own.

1 CORINTHIANS, GALATIANS, AND ROMANS

After discovering the relationship between Paul and the Gospel of Mark through the use of Abba, Dalmatia, and Illyricum, I pulled out my Strong's Concordance, a spiral notebook, and a pencil, and went through Mark one word at a time to see whether the same words and phrases appeared in Paul's authentic letters. I wrote down every word and phrase in Mark that also occurs in Paul. When I finished, I was stunned by how many parallels emerged, and even more stunned that they appeared in a parallel sequence. I remain amazed that no one has done this with a computer; a digital search or AI analysis. If they did I am sure that they would likely uncover even more connections than I found by hand.

For this comparison, I focus on the letters most scholars agree came from Paul: Galatians, 1 Corinthians, and Romans. These letters reflect the teachings Paul delivered to the churches he founded, and the earliest hearers of Mark's Gospel would have recognized the language and themes echoed by the rhapsode.

I begin with 1 Corinthians. I identified three sets of parallels between 1 Corinthians and the Gospel of Mark, each set is remarkable not only for its content but for the fact that the parallels appear in the same sequence in both texts.

1 CORINTHIANS

Set One

1. Secrets: Paul writes about a secret wisdom of God (1 Cor 2:7). Mark writes that the disciples have been given the secret to the kingdom of God (Mark 4:11a).
2. Perceiving: Paul writes about those who are on the outside as not perceiving (1 Cor 2:14). Mark writes about those on the outside everything is in parables that they might see but not perceive (Mark 4:11b).
3. Hidden things: Paul writes about the Lord bringing to light the things now hidden (1 Cor 4:5b). Mark writes about the lamp under a bushel and that there is nothing that is hidden that will not be made manifest (Mark 4:21–25).
4. Eating food: Paul writes about eating food in honor of gods in that food does not make us better and does not make us worse but the appearance of eating it as offered to a god could offend (1 Cor 8:1–13). Mark writes about keeping traditions when we eat whereas it is not the food that defiles a person but rather what a person does that defiles him (Mark 7:1–23).
5. Warnings: Paul writes that God was not pleased with many who followed Moses, and that their fate serves as a warning for us (1 Cor 10:1–6). Mark writes that this generation will not be given the sign or warning (Mark 8:11–13).

Set Two

1. Death and Resurrection of Jesus: Paul writes about the death and resurrection of Jesus (1 Cor 15:1–4). Mark has Jesus tell his disciples about his impending death and resurrection (Mark 9:30–32).
2. The Least: Paul writes that he is the least of the apostles (1 Cor 15:9). Mark writes that whoever would be first must be last and servant of all (Mark 9:33–35).
3. Whoever does it: Paul makes a point of no matter who it was that preached, you believed (1 Cor 15:10–11). Mark has Jesus say, "Whoever is not against us is for us," and praises even the one who gives a cup of water (Mark 9:38–41).
4. Discourse on hell: Paul has a rather lengthy discourse on hell (1 Cor 15:12–58). Mark also discusses hell (9:42–50).
5. Traveling: Paul writes about traveling to Jerusalem (1 Cor 16:1–4). Mark writes about Jesus traveling to Judea beyond the Jordan—the route toward Jerusalem (Mark 10:1).

Set Three

1. Chastised Corinthians and Priests: Paul chastises the Corinthians for creating divisions at the Lord's supper (1 Cor 11:17–34). Mark chastises the priests neglecting the purpose of the temple, a house of prayer for all (Mark 11:17).
2. Temple for all people: Paul wrote that all people are part of the same body—all nations (1 Cor 12:12–13). Mark writes that the temple is the house of prayer for all people/nations (Mark 11:17).
3. Faith to move mountains: Paul writes in one of the most quoted chapters in the bible that even if we have the faith to move mountains (1 Cor 13:2). Mark writes that whoever has faith and says to this mountain (Mark 11:22).

4. The greatest is love: Paul writes that there are three, faith, hope and love and the greatest is love (1 Cor 13:13). Mark has Jesus declare that the greatest commandment is to love God, and the second is like it: to love one's neighbor (Mark 12:28–31).

No scholar has proposed the sequential parallels between Mark and Paul's letters that I outline here. While some have noted thematic similarities or Pauline influence on Mark, none have traced these specific comparisons or argued that Mark's narrative reflects the structure of Paul's teaching. The connections presented here are my own.

I found it incredible that the Last Supper words in 1 Corinthians (11:23–26) and the Gospel of Mark (14:22–25) differ so sharply. Equally striking is that Mark and Matthew (26:26–29) are nearly identical, while 1 Corinthians and Luke (22:17–20) share the language of remembrance, which Mark and Matthew do not.

I included the above paragraph to show that I am not forcing evidence to fit a predetermined conclusion. These differences raise questions that scholars beyond my understanding will need to address.

MARK AND ROMANS

Mark also draws from Paul's epistle to the Romans and Galatians. I had already mentioned the one about Abba and the use of Illyricum and Dalmanoutha but there are two more from Romans. One is basically the theme of both the letter and the gospel; in Romans we are justified by faith and in Mark faith makes us whole.

The other use of Romans by Mark is through a person by the name of Rufus. In the gospel, Rufus is mentioned as the son of Simon of Cyrene (Northern Africa, modern day Libya), "And they compelled a passer-by, Simon of Cyrene, who was coming in from the country, the father of Alexander and Rufus, to carry the cross" (Mark 15:21). Rufus appears again in Paul's letter to the

Romans, where Paul writes, "Greet Rufus, chosen in the Lord, and his mother and mine" (Rom 16:13).

Many scholars focus on whether the woman Paul mentions was his biological mother or someone who cared for him like a mother. That may be an interesting question, but it should not distract from the presence of Rufus. His name would have carried meaning for the church Paul was addressing, and I believe the author of Mark knew this connection. This is why Mark identifies Simon of Cyrene as "the father of Alexander and Rufus."

Seen in this light, the mention of Rufus invites us to revisit the pattern of fathers in Mark's gospel: Jesus and Abba, the Father and Son; James and John, the sons of Zebedee, whom Mark pointedly calls sons of thunder; Bartimaeus, the son of Timaeus—whose name in Greek means honored; and Rufus, son of Simon of Cyrene, whose father carried the cross.

This recurring motif of fathers and sons is not accidental. It reflects a narrative shaped by Paul's communities, Paul's language, and Paul's relationships, including the family of Rufus.

MARK AND GALATIANS

Just one mention of a similarity in the letter to the Galatians and Mark. In the gospel we have Jesus associating with tax collectors and sinners eating a meal with them: "When the Pharisees saw this they said to his disciples 'Why does he eat with tax collectors and sinners'" (Mark 2:15, 16)? In Galatians 2:1–21, Paul confronts the Judaizers over the same issue: table fellowship and the boundaries of belonging. Paul (and Peter) ate with Gentiles, an act that, while not explicitly forbidden in the Hebrew Scriptures, had become culturally unacceptable because of Jewish concerns about purity, food dedicated to other gods, and diet. Josephus wrote that Jews avoided contact with other peoples because of their separateness (*Against Apion* 1.60). Paul exposes the contradiction directly: "If you, though a Jew, live like a Gentile and not like a Jew, how can you compel the Gentiles to live like Jews" (Gal 2:15b)?

I have observed that Mark does not just reflect Paul's ideas; he turns Paul's specific letters into a living narrative. From the Rufus connection in Romans to the table fellowship in Galatians, the Gospel of Mark acts as a witness to the theology Paul fought for in Asia Minor.

3

Mark Used for a Baptism Ritual

THIS CHAPTER EXPLORES HOW the Gospel of Mark may have been used as a baptismal ritual in the early church. I propose that candidates for baptism were instructed through the actions and words of Jesus, using his journey as a map for their own transformation.

Mark structures his Gospel with a bookend–insertion pattern that would have guided baptismal candidates. The bookends are Jesus' baptism by John and his death on the cross. The insertion is his transformation on the Mount of Transfiguration. These bookends reveal the purpose of the center: just as believers are baptized into Jesus' death, they are promised the same transformation he experienced on the mountain. Because Jesus died for all who follow, baptism becomes the doorway into that new life.

The initiates would understand that they were entering the kingdom of God just as Jesus declared: "The time is fulfilled, and the kingdom of God is at hand" (Mark 1:15). Jesus ushered this kingdom into the world so that anyone could become part of it. Luke echoes this internal reality when he has Jesus say, "The kingdom of God is within you" (Luke 17:21).

Although the gospel was likely used in its entirety for the ritual, I am highlighting what I believe were the most important themes Mark brought to the Pauline churches. He wanted the initiates to understand that, through the ritual, they were stepping into Jesus' journey as they entered the community of faith.

The candidates would be taught that John the Baptizer preached a baptism of change to release the burden of sin. While the common translation is "repentance for the forgiveness of sins," the original Greek suggests a different intent. The word *metanoia* (μετάνοια) means a "change of mind or a change of direction," and *aphesis* (αφεσις) means "a release or letting go of a burden." Since Paul taught that the law can only condemn, these words likely signaled a release from the restrictions of the law. The candidates were being asked to embrace God's kingdom through faith and compassion rather than through legalism.

After his baptism, Jesus was sent into the wilderness, where he was tempted, comforted by angels, and lived among the wild beasts.

THE WILDERNESS

Initiates would be taught that they, too, would face trials that might cause them to reconsider the cost of doing God's will. They might face temptations from friends or family urging them to turn back—much like Peter tempted Jesus. They would understand that entering the faith could put their lives in peril. At the time Mark was written, Christians were being persecuted by Rome, a danger symbolized by Jesus being with the wild beasts. In these trials, they would take comfort in the angels of their community—the brothers and sisters in the faith who provided them care and served as symbols of divine protection.

THE TRANSFIGURATION

During the ritual, the story of the Transfiguration would be central: "Let us make three booths, one for you and one for Moses and one for Elijah" (Mark 9:5). When the voice from the cloud declares, "This is my beloved Son; listen to him" (Mark 9:7–8), the initiates were being taught a clear lesson: Jesus is the sole leader of their faith. Moses (the Law) and Elijah (the Prophets) appear at first, but they ultimately fade away, leaving only Jesus as the authority to be followed.

The wilderness trials and the transformation on the mount foreshadowed the difficult choices Jesus would make, a path the initiates might be called to follow in their own lives. While the legalization of Christianity in 313 CE may seem like a short time on paper, the lived experience of early Christians was one of recurring sacrifice and courage for nearly two hundred and fifty years.

For Jewish initiates, this transformation meant leaving behind the law and its exclusionary boundaries to embrace a new understanding: that through faith, all are one and co-heirs with Christ. It also meant a departure from the traditional prophetic call; rather than a "return" to the old ways, it was a call to embrace the new kingdom. For Greek initiates, it meant turning away from the philosophies and religious practices of their youth to take up a mantle of faith and love without qualification.

The Mount of Transfiguration thus becomes the hinge between baptism and death, the moment when identity, purpose, and direction are clarified.

THE DEATH

At the crucifixion, Jesus cries out, "My God, my God, why hast thou forsaken me" (Mark 15:34)? As he prepared to breathe his last, he was utterly alone; his friends had fled to avoid sharing his fate. To fulfill the will of God, he had to experience this death on behalf of all who would follow him through baptism. After he breathed his last, a Roman centurion proclaimed, "Truly this man was the Son of God" (Mark 15:39). This pagan centurion saw what the disciples themselves could not.

In the baptismal ritual, as the initiate rose from the water, a member of the community would likely echo the centurion's words: "Truly, you are a son of God." This affirmation sealed the initiate's transformation and served as a public confession of their new identity within the community of faith.

FURTHER INSTRUCTIONS

The Gospel of Mark echoes Paul's foundational teachings: that "there is neither Jew nor Greek" (Gal 3:28), that the message is "to the Jew first but also to the Greek" (Rom 1:16), and that "those who were not my people I will call my people" (Rom 9:25). The initiates would have heard these themes dramatized when Jesus redefined the very concept of family: "Who are my mother and my brothers? . . . Whoever does the will of God is my brother, and sister, and mother" (Mark 3:33–35). Through this, they understood that anyone marginalized by the law, symbolized by the leper, the woman with the issue of blood, and the young girl—was welcomed into the community of faith exactly as they were.

The candidate for baptism would spend considerable time learning the nature of Jesus. They would be taught that their resources were now meant to assist those in need, providing essentials without regard to social differences—just as Jesus did in the two feeding narratives. This embodied the early church's commitment to communal care and to those who were vulnerable. They would come to understand that while faith brought them into the community, it was the compassion shown to them, regardless of status, that would sustain them on their journey.

Their baptism in water symbolized a deliberate choice to walk a path leading to the will of God. Jesus called for a transformation from their former lives to a new way of living marked by inclusion and unconditional love. As I understand it, Jesus died for preaching this ideal way of life, and all who followed him were called to move from the common world into this ideal kingdom.

This time of learning reached its climax after the Lord's Supper. There, the initiates were told that through their lives, Jesus would drink again of the "fruit of the vine . . . anew in the kingdom of God" with them (Mark 14:25). Finally, after understanding the peril that accompanied this choice, the candidates would withdraw in prayer. In that moment of quiet, they would pray to Abba, just as Jesus did in Gethsemane: "Not my will, but yours be done" (Mark 14:36).

THE RITE OF BAPTISM

Mark provides a striking glimpse into how the early church may have conducted its baptisms. An elder would introduce the initiates to the congregation, explaining that they, like Jesus, had prayed to Abba (Mark 14:36). This was a declaration that they would no longer act according to their own preferences, but according to the will of God.

The initiates then underwent a symbolic act of disrobing, just as the young man in the garden did: "And a young man followed him, with nothing but a linen cloth about his body; and they seized him, but he left the linen cloth and ran away naked" (Mark 14:51–52). The guards represented the authority of the temple and the law; the removal of the garment symbolized a complete release from that religious and cultural grip.

Next, the initiates were led before the elders for questioning, just as Jesus stood before the priests (Mark 14:53–65). They were asked if they were children of the Blessed. Because they had prayed to Abba, they could answer with a confident, I am, acknowledging their status as joint heirs with Christ.

Finally, the primary elder would present the candidate to the church for a vote of inclusion. He would ask the assembly, "Then what shall I do with the man whom you call the King of the Jews?" and the crowd would respond, "Crucify him" (Mark 15:12–13). In this symbolic moment, the church voted no to Caesar and asked that Barabbas be released.

The candidates, as the new Barabbas, would be released while their old self was symbolically taken away to be "crucified" under the water. When the initiates emerged, a white garment was placed upon them, signaling their rebirth.

When the assembly, symbolizing the crowd, shouted for the king of the Jews to be crucified and for Barabbas to be released, they were making a radical theological claim: Jesus the Christ is Lord. Such a confession directly challenged Nero, who claimed absolute lordship over the Roman Empire. In that world, acknowledging Jesus as Lord placed an initiate in immediate jeopardy. Later, leaders like Ignatius of Antioch would be executed in Rome for this very refusal to renounce their faith or sacrifice to Roman idols.

Once they emerged from the baptismal waters, the initiates were taken to a symbolic tomb to reflect on the gravity of their choice. There, they would announce to the church that Jesus was not there, that he had gone before them. This brings us to the mysterious ending of Mark: the women who hear the words of the young man in the tomb flee in terror (Mark 16:6–8).

Why did they run away? Because the young man's message, "He has gone before you," carried a heavy price. It meant that anyone who follows must "deny themselves and take up their cross" daily (Mark 8:34). The women and the disciples knew that Jesus's path ended on a Roman cross; to follow him meant they had to own that cross as their own and possibly face the same consequence. The fear at the end of Mark is the honest realization of what it truly means to be a Christian in a hostile empire.

Ever since the recording of Jesus' death on a cross, the Jews have been condemned for having caused it. But the government of Rome executed Jesus. The crowd that followed him chose the release of Barabbas. The people who came to him for healing were Jews; the people who flocked to hear him speak were Jews; and though the priests of his religion were angered with him, they did not kill him.

WHAT DID BAPTISM ORIGINALLY MEAN?

In the early church, baptism was more than an initiation; it was a symbolic gesture of a candidate's acceptance of Paul's theology that all are one in Christ.

Today, Christianity has evolved from a small, radical sect into a global religion, with denominations shaping its many expressions. As a result, baptism—once a bold declaration of faith often accompanied by profound personal sacrifice—has in many places become a cultural rite of passage. It is now frequently seen as an expected step within a community rather than the radical, life-altering break from one's past that it originally signified.

As this manuscript has shown, Mark shares a deeply intentional relationship with Paul. This connection is visible not only in narrative figures like Barabbas and geographical references such as *Dalmanoutha* and Illyricum, but also in the structural and thematic parallels to 1 Corinthians, Galatians, and Romans. Most importantly, it appears in the ritual of baptism itself—a ceremony designed to transform the initiate into a son of the Father and a co-heir with Christ, ready to face the world with the same courage as the one who went before them.

PAUL AND BAPTISM

Although Paul does not describe his own baptism in his letters—the Acts of the Apostles records it as the climax of his conversion. On the road to Damascus, he was halted by a voice: "Saul, Saul, why do you persecute me?" Paul replied, "Who are you, Lord?" and the voice answered, "I am Jesus, whom you are persecuting" (Acts 9:4–5). After three days of blindness and prayer, a disciple named Ananias, acting on a divine vision, laid his hands on Saul. His sight was restored, and he was immediately baptized.

For Paul, baptism was a profound symbolic commitment. In his letter to the Romans, he teaches that it marks the threshold of a new existence, calling converts to "walk in newness of life" (Rom 6:4). Yet in 1 Corinthians, Paul expresses a surprising reservation: "I am thankful that I baptized none of you except Crispus and Gaius. . . For Christ did not send me to baptize but to preach the gospel" (1 Cor 1:14–17).

Paul's concern was that converts were becoming distracted by who performed the ritual, potentially drifting away from the core message. Was he worried that the "circumcision party" was involved (Gal 2–12). It was connected to James and the Jerusalem leadership which might pull his converts back toward the very legalistic boundaries he believed Christ had abolished? For both Paul and the author of Mark, baptism was never merely a ritual act. It was the beginning of a transformed life, a new allegiance, and a radical new identity within the community of Christ. It would be a life of practice and not merely belief: "If I have faith, so as to remove mountains, but have not love, I am nothing" (1 Cor 13:2b).

THE CHURCH TODAY

The church of today has often drifted from Paul's original intent, returning to a religion of laws, boundaries, and requirements. Paul warned the Galatians, "You are severed from Christ, you who would be justified by the law" (Gal 5:4a). For him, baptism was not a ritual of belonging to an institution but a decisive change of direction—away from reliance on the law and toward faith, grace, and the conviction that all are one in Christ.

Yet in many places the church has become ritualistic in its practice of baptism and communion. These rites, once symbols of transformation and courage, are often treated as formalities. The early church understood baptism as a release from old identities and a new allegiance to Christ; today it is frequently approached as an expected step within a community rather than the radical, life-altering commitment it originally signified.

Paul and Mark both envisioned a community where faith expressed itself through love, where the marginalized were welcomed, and where the law no longer determined who was worthy. Recovering that vision does not require abandoning ritual, but restoring the transformation it was meant to signify.

4

Judeo-Christian or Greek-Christian

WHEN THE TERM JUDEO-CHRISTIAN first appeared in the early nineteenth century, it referred specifically to Jews who had converted to Christianity. Over time, mainstream usage has come to treat the term as if it describes a natural continuum from Judaism to Christianity. The structure of the Bible, with the Old Testament placed before the New Testament, reinforces this impression. Some Bibles also include the Apocrypha, a collection of texts centered on Judah's history, the Temple, and the priesthood. For that reason, I prefer to separate the testaments—Hebrew scriptures for the Jews and Christian scriptures for Christians.

A Roman Catholic priest uses readings at Mass that include one from the Hebrew scriptures and two from the Christian scriptures. In Protestant churches, sermons are based on either the Hebrew or Christian scriptures. The Christian liturgical calendar includes suggested readings from the Old Testament, Psalms, Epistles, and Gospels. These practices suggest that theologians view Christianity as a growth out of Judaism.

Conservative Christians often advocate for the Ten Commandments to be posted on public property. These practices reinforce the idea of a Judeo-Christian continuum. Yet I believe such a concept did not exist in the early church. Instead, there was a more pronounced confrontation between Jewish law and Greek philosophy.

Through this study I have come to see that Christianity was shaped more by the Greek than the Judeo, even though Jesus, John, James, Peter, and Paul were all Jews. Yet the voice from heaven at the Transfiguration clearly separates Jesus from the Law and the Prophets. When I dug deeper, I found that many assumptions we take for granted force us to reconsider Christianity's actual relationship with first-century Judaism.

It is important to revisit a well-known verse, Romans 1:16, where Paul states that the Jew is first and also the Greek (*Hellēni*, Ἕλληνι). What is Paul saying? Is he defending the legitimacy of his Greek converts, and by extension the legitimacy of what would become the Christian movement? *Hellas* (Ἑλλάς) refers to ancient Greece in its broadest sense, encompassing not only modern Greece but also western and southwestern Asia Minor, the islands between, and Macedonia to the north. Paul evangelized much of this region, as the Christian scriptures attest: Corinth, Galatia, Ephesus, Philippi, Thessalonica, and Colossae. Likewise, John's Revelation addresses seven churches in Asia Minor—Smyrna, Pergamum, Thyatira, Sardis, Philadelphia, and Laodicea.

It is striking, then, that we possess so little information about the Christian churches in Judea.

Despite his extensive outreach, Paul faced challenges in maintaining theological unity. He notes in Galatians (1:7a) that someone was preaching "another gospel," offering a competing theology. While the identity of this rival remains unclear, one might question whether figures like James, John, or Peter could have played that role. After all, the Christian scriptures provide little evidence of these disciples evangelizing beyond the accounts in Acts and possibly the letters of James, Timothy, and Titus (though all three were likely written after the deaths of the disciples). Did this silence reflect theological tensions or differing approaches among early church leaders? Or was it a sign of the growing Greek influence and the decline of Jewish traditions?

Although Jesus and his disciples were from Judah, Paul, a Jew, was from Tarsus (Acts 9:11b), located on the southern coast of Asia Minor near Lystra. Christian tradition places the gospel stories in first-century Israel, but Mark's use of *Dalmanoutha* and Abba, as well as his parallels to Paul, suggests that the author is making the gospel Jesus more like Paul in his efforts to evangelize *Hellas*. This points to Mark's author being from *Hellas*, with Paul influencing the author's theology (or vice versa), incorporating Greek myth, Greek tragedy, and the Hebrew scriptures into the gospel.

One enduring ritual across Christian denominations is the celebration of the Last Supper—Communion. The first communion meal Jesus offered to his disciples was at Passover, but Mark's account does not describe it as a Seder meal. The only edibles mentioned were bread (not specified as unleavened), the sop they dipped it in, and wine. A first-century Seder meal would have lamb, unleavened bread, bitter herbs, a hard-boiled egg, dried fruit and/or nuts, and wine, though the exact elements depended on what was available. Mark's portrayal of the meal invites speculation; was the author subtly weaving his own culture into this pivotal moment? That he did not have Jesus mention anything about the Exodus should raise questions.

There were two Greek festivals that honored the gods who provided the bread and wine. They were the most revered gods, even more than Zeus—Demeter and Dionysus.

Demeter, the goddess of grain, had a festival in the fall after the harvest, which was celebrated in secret (unlike the festival of Dionysus). It was held with both joy and sadness: joy for the harvest, but sadness as Demeter and her daughter Persephone would leave until their return in the spring, when the grain was planted again.

The celebration of Dionysus was held in the spring as a symbol of renewal and the cycle of life. He was even given the title "god of the resurrection." His triumph over death was central to their understanding of hope and continuity, especially in their agricultural society. Similarly, the resurrection of Jesus in the spring, as depicted in the Gospels, offered spiritual renewal and eternal life. This thematic parallel likely made Jesus' story more accessible to Greeks, as it echoed familiar cultural narratives while introducing a new theological dimension. By drawing on these shared motifs, early Christian evangelists could bridge cultural divides, helping Greeks see Jesus not as a foreign figure but as a fulfillment of concepts they already cherished.

The Last Supper's bread and wine in Mark would be understood by the ancient Greeks, and John's Gospel might help us understand why: "I am the resurrection and the life" (John 11:25). Consider these parallels: both Dionysus and Jesus were celebrated in the spring, both were sons of gods, both experienced resurrection, and both offered hope to the people.

The Greeks, especially the Epicureans and Stoics, believed the gods acted according to an unchangeable divine order. Epicureans saw the gods as remote and uninvolved, while Stoics taught that fate was fixed and the wise person accepted it. Their prayers were not attempts to persuade the gods but expressions of aligning themselves with what could not be changed. In contrast, the Hebrew scriptures portray a God who listens, responds, and can be petitioned,—a God who may change course. Jesus' prayer in Gethsemane, "Take this cup from me; yet not my will but yours be done," begins in the Jewish tradition of prayer but ends in a surrender that would have sounded deeply Greek. Mark's audience would have recognized the language immediately.

Paul's relationship with his Greek past can be seen in his writings about the afterlife, which is not prominent in the Hebrew Scriptures but was central to Greek philosophy. Pythagoras (500s BCE) is remembered as teaching reincarnation and a blessed afterlife, concepts similar to the Christian notion of heaven. Additionally, Greek thought viewed the physical body as the soul's temple, echoed in Paul's declaration: "Do you not know that the body is the temple of the Holy Spirit?" (1 Cor 6:19). Such phrasing may have been particularly meaningful to Greek converts, reinforcing their understanding of spiritual transformation.

The Greek influence can also be seen in 1 Corinthians: "For now we see in a mirror dimly, but then face to face" (13:12), a line that resonates with Plato's cave allegory. In that story, Socrates describes prisoners who see only shadows of reality on the cave wall. Once released, their sight adjusts to the light outside, allowing them to perceive the true forms that cast the shadows, finally "face to face." Both metaphors describe a movement from partial understanding to ultimate truth, whether spiritual, as Paul presents it, or philosophical, as in Plato's vision. Paul's reference to a "dim mirror" would have been immediately recognizable to his audience, who used polished bronze mirrors that offered imperfect reflections. His words likely carried special meaning for Greek converts, who would have heard echoes of their own philosophical heritage in his portrayal of enlightenment.

Both Hebrew and Greek traditions used fire to signify the presence of the divine. In Acts, tongues of fire rest on the apostles at Pentecost, symbolizing the presence of the Holy Spirit (Acts 2:1–2). The Stoics likewise saw fire as the essence of the divine, the creative force animating the cosmos. The Hebrew Scriptures portray God in the burning bush (Exod 3:2–4) and the pillar of fire (Exod 13:21). These shared symbols created a bridge of understanding for Greek converts encountering the Christian message.

Among the many healers in Greek mythology, Aesculapius stands out for his power to heal the sick and even raise the dead, themes that would have made Jesus' miracles immediately intelligible to Greek audiences. Aesculapius himself was executed and later restored to life, reinforcing the idea that divine power triumphs over death. These stories would help explain how Mark could convince Gentile converts to believe in Jesus' healing stories and his resurrection.

These similarities strengthen the argument that Jesus shares much in common with Greek cultural and philosophical traditions. Beyond Aesculapius, connections can be drawn to Prometheus and Aeneas, as well as Demeter, Dionysus, and Plato. Each figure reflects elements of healing, sacrifice, resurrection, or philosophical depth that resonate with the narratives in the Christian

Scriptures. By weaving these threads together, it becomes clear how early Christianity could bridge the Greek and Jewish worlds, offering a theology that appealed to diverse cultural perspectives.

The early tensions between the Greek and the Jew, as well as the apparent differences separating Paul from James and John, are pivotal to understanding the dynamics of the early church. These distinctions further provide crucial context for interpreting the events in Acts. For instance, the accusation leveled against Stephen by members of the non-Greek synagogues reflect a broader cultural and theological rift. Stephen's defense, that the temple would be destroyed and rebuilt without hands, promoted faith over the law and challenged the authority of the priesthood. This same divide appears in Paul's later writings, where he argues that adherence to the law, such as circumcision, nullifies the transformative power of Jesus' sacrifice. "If you let yourselves be circumcised, Christ will be of no value to you" (Gal 5:2). Here, Paul contrasts faith with the law, directly confronting the legalism upheld by the priests.

Of the many things that compare the Greek and the Jew is the idea that Jesus is declared the Son of God at his baptism in all four Gospels. He is also declared the Son of God at the Transfiguration in the Gospels of Matthew, Mark, and Luke.

If we read the Hebrew and Christian scriptures from cover to cover, we will find that the son or sons of God appear in both, with the exception of Mark's use of Abba and the birth narratives in Matthew and Luke. The term is mostly used for a favored or special person, such as Moses, the people he led out of Egypt, David, or Solomon. However, we cannot ignore the words from the garden scene where Jesus prays to Abba, which marks a difference in the relationship of Jesus as being someone other than a favored or special person of God. Although the birth narratives of Matthew and Luke are similar to that of Samson's, the idea that Jesus is God's Son is as Greek as Prometheus being the son of Iapetus, not Judeo as in Moses, David, or Solomon being sons of God.

Among the many differences between Greek and Jewish life, several stand out for understanding the world in which early Christianity took shape. The Greek language was vowel-heavy and expandable; the Hebrew language was consonant-heavy and rigid. The Greeks had city-states that were often at war with one another, even when the Persians were invading, while the Jews were a loose federation of tribes willing to support each other in times of need. Greeks believed in their many gods and held them in high esteem, but religion was not central in their lives; the Jews had one God, an active priest cult, and their religion was very important. The Greeks tolerated same-sex relationships; the Jews did not. The Greek diet was open-ended; the Jewish diet had strict limitations on what one ate and with whom. And finally, circumcision: Paul's inclusion of the uncircumcised created a deep schism between him and the disciples who demanded that the proselytes keep the Law.

Paul evangelized the Greeks, while John, James, and Peter focused on the Jews, which led to theological disagreements and, perhaps, fueled Mark's frustration with the divisions that arose. These differences are evident in Paul's words to the Galatians: "There is neither Jew nor Greek. . . all are one in Christ" (3:28). Ephesians declares, "He has broken down the wall of hostility" (2:14). Mark's call to "Love your neighbor as yourself" (12:31) and John's "Love others as I have loved you" (13:34) further emphasize the theme of unity through compassion. Could the repeated scriptural emphasis on unity through faith in Christ be a response to the divisions that existed within the early church, and a message still relevant for Christians today?

If we think about it, the walls being brought down by Christ are more than just the concept of inclusivity; they signify liberation from restriction and confinement. The divisions of Paul's time were not merely religious disagreements; they were barriers that separated people based on law, culture, and identity. Paul's frustration with the Judaizers stemmed from their insistence that faith must conform to Mosaic Law, reinforcing separation instead of embracing Christ's message of unity and freedom.

The Roman centurion's recognition of Jesus at the cross is an ironic contrast to the rejection Jesus experienced from his own disciples. Paul saw a similar pattern in his mission to the Gentiles, where outsiders often embraced his message more readily than those of his own religion. His declaration to the Galatians that "all are one in Christ" echoes this theme. If faith in Christ removes barriers, then the centurion's moment of insight is a path to the broader movement away from exclusion and toward unshackled inclusion through faith and understanding.

Mark's Gospel and Paul's letters both challenge the idea that faith should be confined within religious walls. Instead of rigid hierarchy, they emphasize a faith that moves freely, allowing people to live and interact without imposed structures of control. By breaking down these barriers, the message of Christ—and Paul's vision for the early church—becomes one of movement, liberation, and clarity rather than confinement.

In reflecting on "Love your neighbor as yourself" (Mark 12:31), many interpret this command as simply liking or tolerating one another. However, its deeper meaning calls us to compassion, an active love that seeks to address the needs of others. This principle was neglected by the non-Greek members of the synagogues when they withheld support from Stephen's Greek members, even though they had the means to help. Their failure to act underscores the importance of love as a transformative force, one that bridges divides and fosters unity. True faith, as exemplified by Christ, is not just belief but compassionate action, reaching beyond differences to meet the needs of all.

5

Who Wrote Mark?

The identity of Mark's author remains a matter of conjecture, as the evidence available to us comes solely from the late first- or second-century church fathers, whose guesses were often educated or biased and based on hearsay rather than eyewitness testimony or written accounts.

Based on what I have explored earlier, I propose that Mark's gospel was written just before or shortly after Paul's execution (circa 64 CE). The church in Dalmatia, in the district of Illyricum, was likely its first recipient. A clue in Paul's own letter, which I will explore later in this chapter, suggests that Mark was already being composed before Paul's journey to Rome, and that Paul himself was aware of how the work was taking shape.

My argument is rooted more in circumstantial than concrete evidence: the gospel's content points to an author who had access to Paul's letters to the Corinthians, Galatians, and Romans. Romans, in particular, suggests that this individual was with Paul in Dalmatia before his journey to Rome and may even have accompanied him there. The author's use of the term *Dalmanoutha* alongside Paul's references to Illyricum strikes me as too specific to be accidental.

So, who was the author? Before naming my candidate, it's important to note that Luke is the most confidently identified gospel author, as well as Paul being widely regarded as the author of 1 and 2 Corinthians, Galatians, and Romans. However, all other entries in the Christian scriptures face questions regarding authorship.

Scholars examining the Bible often feel compelled to explore and debate these possibilities. Many attribute the Gospel of Mark to Peter's companion and friend—some say his nephew—John Mark. Yet I believe the evidence suggests otherwise. Would someone so close to Peter write passages that have Jesus call him Satan (Mark 8:33), rebuke him for denying Jesus (Mark 14:66–72), describe him as being asleep during a critical moment in Gethsemane (Mark 14:37), and even imply that he was on the outside of the kingdom (Mark 4:10–14)? Such unflattering portrayals suggest that the author may not have been John Mark, but rather someone with a contentious view of Peter, perhaps even contempt.

I propose that the author of Mark was an educated and wealthy individual, someone with access to a library and a deep familiarity with Greek tragedy, Roman literature, and the Hebrew scriptures. This is evident in the Gospel's references to works such as *Prometheus Bound* and the *Aeneid*, as well as its connections to figures and themes from Abraham and Ezekiel. Such an individual would likely have employed a rhapsode to orally convey the gospel to Paul's churches, an expense only someone of means could afford. Additionally, Paul's noticeable growth in writing skill and conceptual clarity after 1 Thessalonians (assuming he wrote it) suggests the presence of a skilled person. It is possible that someone with strong literary capabilities collaborated on, or even authored, Galatians, Corinthians, and Romans, shaping Paul's ideas into more refined and impactful work. I believe that Mark's author wrote the prison epistles, Ephesians, Philippians, and Colossians.

My candidate for the author of Mark is the person behind the name Philemon, which I believe to be a nom de plume. Paul was in Rome when he wrote his letter to Philemon, the only personal letter we have from him, and this suggests a unique and significant relationship between the two men. Philemon appears to have been wealthy enough to own a slave, as several translations indicate, and wealthy enough to afford the services of a rhapsode—my understanding. These factors, along with the possible wordplay in Paul's letter to Philemon that resembles the linguistic intricacies found in Mark's Gospel, further support my claim about the author's identity.

While I acknowledge that there are Greek scholars far more qualified than I am to translate the Christian scriptures, I believe that Paul's imprisonment in Rome involved critical matters of life and death, and perhaps even reconciliation with Simon Peter. Church history, vague at best, preserves hints of this. Lactantius (*De Mortibus Persecutorum* 2), writing more than two centuries later (313–16 CE), claimed that Peter reconciled with Paul in Rome while he awaited trial. Earlier still, in the second century, writers such as Irenaeus asserted that Peter founded the church at Rome.

Furthermore, the author of the Gospel of Mark, known for portraying Jesus' disciples unfavorably—particularly Peter—provides a fascinating perspective through which to examine Paul's letter to Philemon. In this letter, I read subtle linguistic nuances potentially referencing Simon Peter. For example, traditional translations render the Greek name *Onesimon* (ονεσιμον) as Onesimus, meaning "profitable." These details offer another layer of intrigue to the authorship of Mark, especially since the text indicates that Paul was euphoric that *Onesimon* was returning to Philemon: "I appeal to you for my child, Onesimus, whose father I have become in my imprisonment. (Formerly he was useless to you, but now he is indeed useful to you and to me.) I am sending him back to you, sending my very heart" (1:10–11).

Since the name in the Greek text is not Onesimus but *Onesimon*, I examined the word more closely, I noticed that it contains the element *simon* (σιμον), which immediately suggests the possibility of deliberate wordplay. The name can even be divided in ways that echo this: *ονε σιμον* resembles "*one simon*," and *o ne simon*. The particle *o* can function as "that," and *ne* can carry a negating force in certain contexts—that "un-simon?" I am not claiming to be a Greek scholar, only that the name seems to invite the same kind of linguistic play we see throughout Mark's gospel.

Even if some of these interpretations are speculative, the simple fact that the name contains, *simon*, is striking, a detail that may hint at Peter and, in turn, lend unexpected support to the tradition preserved by Lactantius.

My point is simply that Mark employed wordplay throughout his gospel, as I have already shown, and that Paul may have been aware of this pattern. Was Mark writing the Gospel while he accompanied Paul to Rome?

Although the Christian scriptures offer no definitive evidence that Peter broke from John and James to align with Paul in Rome, the possibility remains. If the name *Onesimon* does carry a deliberate reference to Simon Peter, Paul's letter to Philemon may have been a subtle way of signaling Peter's renewed support. Given Peter's earlier wavering in Galatia, Paul would have welcomed such a shift. It is also possible that Philemon himself remained cautious, aware of Peter's history of changing positions.

Whatever personal mistrust may have lingered, both Peter and Paul were executed during Nero's reign, their deaths occurring close in time. This raises an important question: why would Peter have faced execution if he had not changed his position? His willingness to stand for his convictions, even at the cost of his life, underscores the extraordinary commitment both he and Paul brought to the emerging faith. Their example invites us to reflect on the depth of our own commitments today.

A brief thought about the reasons behind the executions of Paul and Peter. Before Paul's death, Nero was not known for executing people solely for their religious beliefs, though he later persecuted Christians because Christianity was not a legal religion. Paul, however, was unwavering in proclaiming Jesus as Christ the Lord and Lord of all (Rom 10:12). Such a declaration posed a direct challenge to Nero, who was recognized as lord over the Roman Empire. If Peter had aligned himself with Paul's mission, he would have faced the same perilous dilemma: whom would they acknowledge as lord, Nero or Jesus?

This tension recalls the question Pilate posed to Jesus: "Are you the King of the Jews?" Jesus replied, "You say it." My interpretation is that he meant, "You are saying it for yourself." One wonders whether Paul would have offered a similar response if confronted by Roman authority. It is a sobering thought, highlighting both the cost of their unwavering faith and the quiet defiance inherent in choosing Christ over earthly rulers. Will our leaders of today who claim Christianity as their religion act similarly?

There are two intriguing possibilities for the use of Philemon as a pseudonym. One is the renowned Athenian playwright Philemon, who wrote New Comedy in the second century BCE. While I have found no evidence in his works that directly relate to the Gospel, his name may have been appropriated by Paul for its familiarity or cultural resonance.

Another possibility comes from Greek mythology, where Philemon appears in a tale involving Zeus and Hermes. Disguised as travelers, the gods wandered among mortals to test their hospitality. Though many shut their doors on them, an elderly, impoverished couple, Philemon and Baucis, welcomed them into their humble home, offering food and shelter. It is possible that the author of Mark performed a similar act of generosity, welcoming Paul into his home and leaving a lasting impression. Perhaps the name Philemon was a nickname bestowed by Paul himself, reflecting the author's hospitality and kindness.

Paul's journey reflects a profound transformation. According to Galatians 1:23 and Acts 8:3, he once persecuted the early church but experienced his conversion on the road to Damascus (Acts 9:1–9). Afterward, he aligned with John's teachings until the disciples sent him to Greece to spread the gospel, as Acts recounts. While in Galatia, Paul's message evolved, prompting accusations from the Judaizers that he was corrupting their message. What triggered this shift in emphasis? Could it have been Philemon's influence, encouraging Paul to preach faith, hope, and love rather than a strict return to the law?

When Paul and Barnabas visited Lystra, the locals mistook them for Zeus and Hermes (Acts 14:12), a reaction that evokes the myth of Philemon and Baucis, which was deeply rooted in the region. Lystra, located at the southern edge of the district of Galatia, may have been where Paul first encountered the Judaizers. Could it also have been the place where he met Philemon early in his ministry? These intersections of myth, scripture, and culture offer a unique lens through which to explore Paul's evolving message.

6

Who Is On The Inside?

AT THE BEGINNING OF my Introduction, I wrote that most of us read the scriptures through a belief system we inherited long before we ever opened a Bible for ourselves. We're taught that the text is Holy Spirit inspired, that it must be read literally, that it contains no contradictions, and that Jesus was one with the Father from the beginning of creation. These assumptions shape how sermons are preached and how passages from the Hebrew and Christian scriptures are woven together, often without regard for the different authors' own intentions.

One of those inherited beliefs is that Jesus performed miracles in a literal, physical sense—restoring sight, opening ears, strengthening legs, and stopping the flow of blood. But Mark's gospel invites us to look again. The healings are not simply displays of power; they are revelations of who is on the inside and who is on the outside, who sees and perceives and who remains blind and deaf. This chapter is about what those miracles actually are, and why they matter for understanding the peril of being on the outside and the grace of being on the inside.

Early in his ministry Jesus is inside preaching to a crowd gathered round him. Four men brought their paralytic friend to him but couldn't get to the inside for him to be helped. The four were so focused on getting to the inside for their friend that they tore away part of the roof and lowered him down to where he was near Jesus. The first thing Jesus said was, "My son, your sins are forgiven." Why did he say that? Did he know the man prior to this encounter? Jesus knew that the man was a paralytic and because of a strict interpretation of the law was deemed a sinner and untouchable (2:1–12).

Immediately after the healing of the paralytic Jesus is on the inside with some others. One of those tells Jesus that his mother and brothers are "outside" asking for him. How does Jesus respond? To those on the "inside" he says, "Here are my mother and my brothers! Whoever does the will of God is my brother, and sister, and mother" (2:31–35). His relatives—law abiding members of his family—are on the outside and on the inside are those who do the will of God, those who embody faith with compassion.

Following this incident Jesus teaches in parables. In Mark 4:11–12, Jesus says, "To you has been given the secret of the kingdom of God, but for those outside everything is in parables, so that they may indeed see but not perceive, and may indeed hear but not understand." He adds, "lest they should turn again and be forgiven." The concept is that in order to receive forgiveness or release we must move away from the direction we have been going in life. The verb "turn again" is *epistrepsōsin*, (ἐπιστρέψωσιν) and carries the sense of a positive turning back or even a turning toward, but movement is essentially what those on the inside have done and what those on the outside need to do.

Immediately afterward, Jesus begins explaining the parables to his disciples. The text raises an interesting question: if the disciples were truly inside, already part of the kingdom of God, why did Jesus need to explain the parables to them (4:34), given that they had been with him almost from the beginning? They had heard him preach and witnessed his actions, yet they did not perceive, they did not understand, and apparently they did not turn again and be forgiven!

I wrote earlier about the Greek meaning translated as forgiveness is actually a release. Release from what? From the very law that had excluded so many of the people that Jesus welcomed to be with him—the paralytic for instance. The question here is not whether a literal healing occurred, but what Mark wants us to see. The man had been bound to his own life, paralyzed by it, and kept outside the kingdom of God because of the law. After his encounter with Jesus, the paralysis of exclusion is gone. He is released, restored, able to follow and on the inside.

A little later, a woman with an issue of blood comes near Jesus. She only has hope to help her and acts through faith, saying to herself, "If I touch even his garments, I shall be made well" (5:28). She touches only the fringe of his cloak, yet Jesus feels it and tells her that her faith has made her whole. The verb normally translated "made well," *sesōken* (σέσωκέν), can also mean "made whole," and that is what happened. Her monthly flow placed her among the untouchables according to the law (Lev 15:19–30), but Jesus receives her, brings her to the inside, and restores her position in society because of her faith.

A little later, a deaf man with a speech impediment encounters Jesus (7:31–37). Mark describes Jesus placing his fingers in the man's ears and touching his tongue with saliva. The man immediately begins to hear and speak clearly. In Mark's symbolic world, hearing means understanding, and speaking means the ability to proclaim. Once his ears are opened, he can understand; once his tongue is released, he can tell others what life on the inside with Jesus is like. The crowd responds, "He has done all things well; he even makes the deaf hear and the dumb speak." Those who were once excluded are now included, and their very presence becomes a sign of the kingdom in their midst.

When Jesus heals the boy who convulses (9:14–29) the story Mark gives is not so much about the healing but about the disciples—that they are on the outside.

A man had taken his son to the disciples but they weren't able to heal him. He then goes to Jesus and relates the efforts of the disciples to him, he says, "O faithless generation, how long am I to be with you? How am I to bear with you? Bring him to me." He tells the father that all things are possible if a person believes, the father responds, "I believe, help my unbelief." After the boy is healed Jesus enters the house and the disciples ask Jesus why they couldn't perform the healing. He answered that the healing can only be accomplished with prayer (to Abba?). Those closest to him were still outside the will of God, even though they were inside the house.

Prior to the healing of Bartimaeus Jesus was confronted by a man who called him "Good Teacher" and wanted to know how he could inherit eternal life (10:17–23). Jesus responded that only God is good and then asked the man about the commandments, the young man responded, "Teacher, all these I have observed from my youth." Jesus responded that he lacked one thing—"sell what you have, and give to the poor, and you will have treasure in heaven, and come follow me." The man walked away sorrowful because he had many possessions!

Jesus didn't stop, after the man left, he continued, "It is easier for a camel to go through the eye of a needle than for a rich man to enter the kingdom of God." The man asked about eternal life, but Jesus responded that in order to enter it he would have to do something in the present. Matthew echoes this by warning that those who fail to care for the least will not enter the kingdom, and Luke blesses the poor while warning the wealthy who have already received their comfort.

Interestingly, I once heard a sermon about the passage of the camel and the eye of a needle. The preacher said there was a formation in the desert called "the eye of a needle" that took an animal smaller than a camel to get through. For me, that preacher represents the great lengths we go to justify wealth. Many Christians, ancient and modern, have gone to great lengths to treat wealth as a sign of divine favor rather than a spiritual danger. Yet Jesus never softens his words. He warns the wealthy, blesses the poor, and insists that entering the kingdom requires a radical reorientation of one's life in the present.

The next healing stands in clear contrast to the rich man. All of the healings share two things: each person is untouchable according to religious law, and each is brought to the inside and into the kingdom and will of God. Bartimaeus is a blind beggar (10:46–52), the son of Timaeus, whose name means "honor." The rich man had kept the commandments from his youth and was well received in society and religion because of his wealth. Bartimaeus, blind from youth, was excluded from both. Jesus did not ask the rich man to believe, as he did the father of the convulsing boy; he asked whether he kept the law and then advised him to sell all that he had and to follow. Bartimaeus simply asked to see. Jesus granted his request and said, "Your faith has made you whole." The man who once sat outside with nothing to offer now sees, is made whole, and enters the inside of the kingdom; more than that, he follows.

Mark continues the rich man's issue about selling all he has and giving to the poor when he has a scribe, a strict interpreter of the law, ask Jesus which is the greatest commandment (12:28–34). Jesus responds by saying that to love God and neighbor with all that one has and, "There is no commandment greater than these." The scribe responds by agreeing with him and then Jesus says, "You are not far from the kingdom of God." If the scribe is not far what did Jesus mean by that? If we take the gospel seriously, being in the kingdom is not about agreement but about practice, following the will of God.

Mark keeps the rich man in view with the story of the widow in the temple (12:41–44). Jesus watches people placing money into the treasury, some giving large sums, while a widow offers two small copper coins. After she gives her "mite," Jesus says, "Truly, this poor widow has put in more than all the others. . . they gave out of abundance, but she out of her poverty."

There is a story from the early days of the Great Society about a widow in Appalachia who was just as generous. She was to receive a small amount of assistance and was interviewed by reporters. When asked what she planned to do with the money, she replied that she would give it to the poor, of course.

This chapter has been about perceiving and understanding who Jesus is and what the will of God looks like. Those who see but do not perceive and hear but do not understand remain on the outside of the kingdom Jesus is bringing. We can hear sermons and appreciate them but if we don't enter into the will of God we are nothing more than "noisy gongs or clanging cymbals" (1 Cor 13:1b).

According to Mark, the disciples themselves are on the outside. When Jesus tells them he is going to Jerusalem to be killed, Peter rebukes him and Jesus calls him Satan; that "you are not on the side of God but of men" (8:31–33). Jesus says that those on the outside must turn again and be released from the law, but even though the disciples heard him he still had to explain the parables to them. Is the reason that they don't perceive or understand because they were unwilling to change from what they were? The condemning message of Jesus is that they lack faith and apparently don't pray, as seen in their failure to heal the convulsing boy.

One of the twelve betrays him. In Gethsemane, while Jesus prays, the disciples sleep, not merely resting, but failing to grasp what he has told them; that he will be killed in Jerusalem. Judas betrays him, Peter denies even knowing him. None of them are at the cross when he dies. Yet someone is there who recognizes him, a pagan Roman centurion.

The rich man kept the law but failed to do what was required and didn't follow, which would have included him on the inside. The centurion seen what those on the outside never did: that Jesus is the son of God.

7

Other Things Gospel

THIS CHAPTER EXPLORES ELEMENTS in the Gospels that did not fit within the focus of the previous chapters but still deserve closer attention. These observations are not exhaustive; some highlight features especially relevant to my study of Mark, while others consider how the Gospels compare with one another and how they relate, or fail to relate.

THE GENEALOGIES

Mark says nothing about Jesus' life before his encounter with John the Baptist and the Gospel of John traces Jesus back to the Word in the beginning. Matthew and Luke offer genealogies and birth narratives, though they differ from each other in almost every respect except one: both include David.

Matthew begins with Abraham and works his way forward to Mary. He includes five women, each of whom faced situations of shame or social judgment: Tamar, Judah's daughter-in-law who bore him two sons; Rahab, the prostitute of Jericho who hid Caleb; Ruth, who was a Moabite; Bathsheba, who bore David's son; and Mary, who conceived before marriage. The author seems convinced that God works through people who might be deemed unseemly to bring about His will. Matthew mentions Joseph only in relation to Mary, keeping the focus on her and effectively making her the descendant of David, unlike Luke's genealogy which claims Joseph as the heir of David.

Luke begins with Jesus and his stepfather, Joseph, and works backward to Adam the son of God. He lists only male ancestors, omitting the women entirely, including Mary.

THE BIRTH NARRATIVES

The birth narratives share thematic parallels with the story of Samson, who liberated his people from the Philistines. Samson was a Nazirite (Judg 13:5b), while Jesus was called a Nazarene (Matt 2:23), or simply identified as being from Nazareth (Matt 2:23 and Luke 4:34). Matthew draws a connection to Moses, echoing the slaughter of the innocents and Jesus' return from Egypt before delivering his sermon on the mount—a parallel to Moses' escape from Egypt and the giving of the Law.

Matthew records that although Mary, engaged to be married to Joseph, was found to be pregnant—Joseph was not the father. He adds that Joseph was an honorable man and was going to divorce her quietly (1:18, 19). The remainder of his story is about what happens after the angel of the Lord convinces Joseph not to divorce Mary. He gives us the wise men, the flight into Egypt, and the settling of the family in Nazareth after their return.

Luke's account is different (1:26—2:52). The angel of the Lord (Gabriel) appears to Mary rather than Joseph and identifies the source of her pregnancy as the Holy Spirit, which surely means that Joseph was not the father. Luke emphasizes that Joseph was of the house of David, anchoring Jesus in messianic lineage—but if Joseph was not the father, did Luke mislead the recipients of his Gospel? Luke also includes the angel's promise that Jesus will reign over the house of Jacob, which was renamed the house of Israel (Gen 32:28).

According to Luke, the couple had to travel to Bethlehem because the people were required to be enrolled for taxation in the city of the male's lineage, and it was there that Mary delivered Jesus. After eight days Jesus was circumcised and then presented in the temple. Since Luke's gospel was written several years after Paul's death, his inclusion of the circumcision was likely a deliberate statement about the continuing importance of the law—a subtle argument for the requirement Paul had rejected.

At the age of twelve he taught in the temple, after which Luke closes with a quiet image: Jesus was obedient to his parents, and Mary, treasuring the encounters with God's messengers, kept them in silence (2:51b).

What can we understand from these two accounts when considering how Jesus grew up before he began making his own decisions? His parents were honorable, observant of both religious and civic law, and likely created an environment where Jesus was taught to make responsible choices. His mother seems to have been observant and considered what she saw but kept her thoughts close to her heart. These glimpses suggest a household shaped by duty, tradition, and quiet obedience.

JOHN THE BAPTIST AND THE BAPTISM OF JESUS

All four Gospels mention John the Baptist, but they differ in how they depict him.

Matthew describes John chastising the Pharisees and Sadducees. When they meet, John tells Jesus that he should be baptized by him, but Jesus replies that he must be baptized "to fulfill all righteousness" (3:13–15). What did Matthew mean by that? Was he not already righteous? Had he sinned, or been labeled unclean in some way that required cleansing?

Mark keeps the account brief. He has John preach a baptism of repentance for the forgiveness of sins, and then Jesus is baptized. I prefer the translation that has John preach a baptism of change for the release of sins, as this better depicts the intent of Mark.

Luke's account of John is longer and different from the others. He writes about John admonishing the crowds and emphasizes sharing what one has so that those in need may benefit (3:7–14).

This is similar to what happens after he records Peter's sermon in Acts (2:41–45). Luke's description of Jesus' baptism (3:21–22) is almost an afterthought. He mentions that Jesus was baptized, but only after John had been imprisoned. Should we assume John baptized him, or question how that could be if John was already in prison?

John's Gospel presents yet another picture. The priests and Levites question John, but the baptism itself is omitted. The author then writes that Jesus was baptizing at the same time as John (3:22–24). He has the baptizer witness the Spirit of God descend on Jesus and remain. He then has John say, "He on whom you see the Spirit descend and remain is the one who baptizes with the Holy Spirit" (1:33b).

THE WILDERNESS AND THE TEMPTATIONS

Matthew has Jesus being led into the wilderness by the Spirit, where he remains forty days and is tempted. The tempter comes to him with three challenges: "If you are the Son of God. . . command these stones to become bread. . . throw yourself down. . . worship me" (4:1–11).

Mark writes that Jesus is driven into the wilderness by the Spirit, where he is tempted by Satan, is with the wild beasts, and is tended to by angels. My understanding is that Satan's temptation appears later in the Gospel, when Peter insists that Jesus must not go to Jerusalem to be crucified. Jesus responds, "Get behind me, Satan" (8:33). The "wild beasts" refer to those mentioned in the prophecy (Ezek 34:25) where the prophet condemns the religious leaders for allowing the wild beasts to devour the sheep. The angels tending to Jesus recalls the angels who cared for Ishmael, who would become the father of a great nation (Gen 17:20).

Luke's account of the wilderness and the temptations is similar to Matthew's, with only slight differences.

John's Gospel does not include the temptations at all.

Why was Jesus sent to the wilderness? The wilderness was the land beyond Jerusalem's walls, far from the religious center.

Gandhi did something similar when he returned to India from South Africa, traveling through regions far from political power and discovering the depth of need there. Likewise, Jesus found in the wilderness many who were in need, especially those excluded from their religion and society and called untouchable: the lame, the blind, and the deaf.

THE NAMING OF THE TWELVE

Other than Jesus naming James and John, the "sons of thunder," there seems to be nothing out of the ordinary with the naming of the twelve. Most all of us can take note that the naming of the twelve echoes the twelve tribes of Israel. When we compare Mark's list of the twelve with the lists of the other Gospels only Matthew's is similar. Luke replaces Thaddaeus and Simon the Canaanite with Simon Zelotes and Judas brother James. John only has eight apostles but doesn't mention James and John by name.

Mark's Twelve	Matthew's Twelve	Luke's Twelve	John's Disciples
Peter	Simon/Peter	Simon	Andrew
James	Andrew	Andrew	Simon/Peter
John	James	James	Philip
Andrew	John	John	Nathanael
Philip	Philip	Philip	Thomas
Bartholomew	Bartholomew	Bartholomew	Judas son of Simon Iscariot
Matthew	Thomas	Matthew	The sons of Zebedee
Thomas	Matthew	Thomas	
James of Alphaeus	James of Alphaeus	James of Alphaeus	
Thaddaeus	Thaddaeus	Simon Zelotes	
Simon Canaanite	Simon the Canaanite	Judas brother James	
Judas Iscariot	Judas Iscariot	Judas Iscariot	

WHY ARE THERE DIFFERENCES?

If I am a serious student of the Bible, how should I treat these differences? First, I must acknowledge that the lists do not fully agree. Second, I should assume there is a reason and look for it. Bartholomew shifts in and out of the lists, but James, John, and Peter remain consistent, even if John mentions them only as "the sons of Zebedee" (21:2). Were the synoptic authors intentionally echoing the twelve tribes of Israel? If so, John shows no interest in preserving that symbolism.

THE FIG TREE

Along with Mark the cursed fig tree is only in Matthew (21:18–21) but it occurs after the temple cleansing. As I wrote in the plays on word, Mark has the cursed fig tree preceding the temple cleansing and concludes with the withered fig tree after it. Neither Luke nor John have it at all. It's interesting to me that all four Gospels include the temple cleansing but not the cursed fig tree.

THE TEMPLE CLEANSING

Matthew, Mark, and Luke all place the temple cleansing after Jesus enters Jerusalem, just before his execution. John, however, places it at the very beginning of Jesus' ministry, immediately after introducing John the baptizer. He does not include a second cleansing that would align with the other Gospels. This suggests that John either preserved an earlier historical placement or intentionally moved the event because its position served his theological purpose.

There are other differences with the temple event. Matthew and Luke omit "for all nations" and John doesn't mention the house of prayer at all. Matthew includes material not found in Mark:

"And the blind and the lame came to him in the temple, and he healed them. But when the chief priests and the scribes saw the wonderful things that he did, and the children crying out in the temple, 'Hosanna to the Son of David!' they were indignant; and they said to him, 'Do you hear what these are saying?' And Jesus said to them, 'Yes; have you never read, "Out of the mouth of babes and sucklings thou hast brought perfect praise?"'"

Luke (19:45–46) only uses two verses for the cleansing. Why? It's important to the other gospel authors and he is writing to Theophilus ostensibly to give him the more orderly account, so his brief account is disconcerting.

John (2:13–22) rewrites the scene altogether. He includes the selling of oxen and sheep along with pigeons and Jesus making a whip made of cords (which herders used to drive animals), overturning the money changers tables and scattering their coins. Instead of accusing the leaders of the temple that had made it a "den of robbers," he writes that Jesus said, "you shall not make my Father's house a house of trade." After the cleansing, Jesus and the Jews have a confrontation in which he announces that he will destroy the temple and rebuild it in three days.

THE SONS OF THUNDER

Mark is also the only Gospel that refers to James and John as the sons of thunder. In Matthew (4:18–22), Jesus calls James and John as his disciples, telling them they will become fishers of men. Luke (5:9–11) mentions James and John as partners with Simon Peter, later saying that all three left everything to follow Jesus. John (21:1–2) refers to them simply as the sons of Zebedee without naming them. Mark's unique designation casts them in a more volatile, less flattering light than do the other Gospels.

DALMANUTHA

Dalmanutha's sole mention is in Mark, while Matthew's parallel passage (15:39) describes Jesus disembarking at Magadan. Magadan's existence is solely attested in Matthew's Gospel, and its relationship to Dalmanutha remains speculative. The two names appear nowhere else in scripture or ancient geography, leaving their connection uncertain.

BARABBAS AND ABBA

All include Barabbas. Luke is similar to Mark, and Matthew and John are similar in that they agree in portraying Barabbas as a man of questionable character. Barabbas appears suddenly in all four Gospels, a figure with no backstory but a name that echoes Jesus' own prayer in Gethsemane and Paul's teaching about praying to Abba. For some reason the other Gospel authors stay away from this.

UNDERSTANDING JESUS AND THOSE HE ENCOUNTERED

I mentioned the healings of the leper, the woman with the twelve-year flow of blood, and the twelve-year-old girl. All three were marginalized by the law: the leper and the woman were stigmatized as untouchable, and the girl, because of her age, was on the threshold of womanhood and slipping into a second-class status in relation to men.

The leper, knowing he was forbidden to touch anyone, still embraced Jesus after the healing. The woman was likely experiencing her monthly cycle and because of that was deemed untouchable according to the law. She dared only to touch the hem of his garment. The girl was silent and passive, and apparently had just been introduced into womanhood through her first cycle. This moment placed on her the primary purpose in society: to bear children and manage the household.

All three had conditions that excluded them or denied them social standing; the acts of Jesus brought them to the inside of the kingdom of God.

THE FEEDING OF THE THOUSANDS

The feedings of the thousands (Mark 6:30–46 and 8:1–10) are similar in that the crowd had assembled to hear a message from Jesus. In the first feeding, the disciples said to Jesus, "This is a lonely place, and the hour is now late; send them away, to go into the country and villages round about and buy themselves something to eat." He told his disciples (probably James, John, and Peter), "You give them something to eat" (6:37). They asked him how they could do that, he responded by asking how many loaves they had. They came back and said five loaves and two fish—from that Jesus fed them all and all who ate were satisfied. The second feeding is similar, and in both accounts the leftovers exceed what they began with.

Immediately following the first feeding Jesus walks on the water, he tells his disciples, "Take heart, it is I; have no fear" (6:50b). And then Mark writes that the disciples were astounded but their hearts were hardened. This is important because after this Jesus goes on to Gennesaret where he is confronted by the Pharisees because they notice that some of the disciples eat their food without having washed. Jesus responds by quoting Isaiah (29:11), "This people honors me with their lips, but their heart is far from me; in vain do they worship me, teaching as doctrines the precepts of men." And then adds, "You leave the commandment of God, and hold fast the tradition of men" (7:8).

There are other passages between the two feedings of the thousands, but this one meets the standard of the bookends and insertion concept. The bookends are the feedings, and the insertion is the condition of the Pharisees' hearts in that they were hardened and that their worship is empty, shaped more by cultural tradition than by the heart of God!

Mark also uses the two feedings to make a point: the disciples are unable to perceive what is happening though they witnessed it. They marvel at the multiplication of bread and the walking on water, but their hearts remain hardened, far from understanding the heart of God.

We are no different. Our culture has within it bigotry toward people of difference and the right to accumulate wealth. Neither hold up when reading the Gospel of Mark and the words of Paul: "sell what you have and give to the poor. . . and. . . follow" and "The dividing walls of hostility are brought down in Christ."

THE FOUR GOSPELS

The four Gospels each shape Jesus' ministry in its own way. I have long believed that each author wrote to influence the new religion through their presentation of Jesus.

Matthew borrows extensively from Mark, while Luke borrows less, yet the two share similarities that are not found in Mark. John uses only a small amount from Mark.

The four Gospels contain striking differences. As central as the Sermon on the Mount (Matt) or the Sermon on the Plain (Luke) seem, both are absent from Mark and John. Mark emphasizes faith, depicting Jesus breaking the law through compassionate actions; healing on the Sabbath and embracing the unclean—rather than centering his narrative on the Mosaic or new law. In contrast, John's Gospel portrays Jesus as the Word of God, emphasizing his divinity as God incarnate. Matthew and Luke both engage the law, though each shapes it according to their theological aims.

Even though Matthew and Luke share similarities, their versions of the Sermon on the Mount reveal notable differences. Matthew writes that the "poor in spirit" inherit the kingdom of Heaven, while Luke writes that the "poor" inherit the kingdom of God (6:20). Luke's Jesus warns, "Woe to you that are rich, for you have received your consolation" (6:24). By contrast, Matthew makes no direct negative remarks about the rich in his sermon, but underscores the importance of compassion, as his Jesus states that whatever people do for the least, they do for Him. For those who fail to show this love, Jesus warns, "Depart from me, you cursed, into the eternal fire prepared for the devil and his angels" (25:41b). In both Luke and Mark, the widow who gave out of her poverty is praised above those who gave from their wealth (Mark 12:43; Luke 21:4).

Luke, though a companion of Paul early in his ministry, seems to push back against some of Paul's more radical positions. He tells Theophilus that his account is more orderly, and he hints at the continuing significance of the law.

Luke's parable of the Prodigal Son (15:11–32) reflects God's unconditional love along with forgiveness, with the emphasis on repentance. The Prodigal's life away from the father may suggest a deeper message aimed not at a single son but at the people as a whole. The Roman occupation may have been understood as a sign that the nation had strayed from God and the Law, and as a call for repentance and restoration.

The prophet Hosea's own marriage became a living parable of God's longing for Israel to return, a theme that echoes through Luke's Prodigal Son. "When the Lord first spoke through Hosea, the Lord said to Hosea, 'Go, take to yourself a wife of harlotry and have children of harlotry, for the land commits great harlotry by forsaking the Lord'" (1:2).

8

Final Thoughts

In this work, I have explored what I call the wordplays, identified Barabbas and Bartholomew, uncovered the reasoning behind Jesus cursing the fig tree, interpreted the meaning of the sons of thunder, located the district of *Dalmanoutha*, and explained the significance of the naming of the twelve disciples. I have demonstrated the author's use of *Prometheus Bound*, the *Aeneid*, and Paul's first letter to the Corinthians, each appearing in Mark in almost the same sequence as the originals. Furthermore, I have shown how Mark drew from Galatians and Romans. I have argued that Christianity, as presented in Mark, owes more to Greek cultural influences than to Hebrew traditions, and I have attempted to identify the author of Mark as Philemon.

Altogether, my findings involve over one hundred verses from Mark, as well as numerous references from Paul's authentic letters. While any one connection might be dismissed as coincidental, the collective weight of these patterns and parallels, all within a single gospel, demands deeper consideration. If nothing else, these patterns invite us to reconsider how the earliest Christian authors shaped their narratives. The Gospel of Mark, in particular, may reflect a more complex cultural and literary world than we often assume.

THE NEED FOR A HISTORICAL JESUS

Within Christianity, there has long been a need to justify the holiness of the Bible and affirm that the Jesus of the gospels aligns with the historical figure. In one notable instance, a group of biblical scholars in the 1990s, known as the Jesus Seminar, convened twice a year to evaluate the authenticity of words attributed to Jesus in the gospels. They employed a system of four colored beads, ranging from "probably authentic" to "not authentic," to cast their votes. Like many others, these scholars questioned whether the Jesus depicted in the gospels truly reflected the historical figure. Yet how can anything be established as fact nearly two thousand years after the events, with minimal corroborating evidence through decisions made through a voting system?

The same type of process occurred when the Bible, as we know it today, was canonized. Comprising both the Hebrew scriptures and the Christian scriptures, it did not begin to take shape until roughly three hundred years after the last Gospel was written, during the Councils of Rome, Hippo, and Carthage. It was not officially closed until the Council of Trent in 1563 when it affirmed what the earlier councils had already accomplished. Remarkably, the votes at the Council of Trent, that determined the canon were cast by a minority of those with the authority to vote—abstentions and nays outnumbered the yeas! The vote at this council is still being debated; this is one of the positions.

I take issue with the process of determining something as significant as what Jesus may have actually said or did, or what is considered holy, through the simple act of people long after the fact casting votes without firm evidence. First, we must account for the centuries separating Jesus, Paul, and the Gospel authors from the various councils. Second, there is little to no documentation to substantiate many of these conclusions. The irony, of course, is that in this manuscript I have become a council of one, the sole voter on what I believe Mark reveals.

There have been many councils throughout Christian history for various reasons beyond the Bible's canonization. Early in

Christianity a council was held to determine the date of Easter, which failed because of the differences in the churches present. In the fourth century at the council of Nicaea, the members sought to define universal beliefs among the disparate churches: Western Catholicism, Anglican, Eastern Orthodox, and Asian Orthodox, for instance. We still live with their conclusions.

THE HISTORICAL JESUS

An essential challenge in exploring the historical Jesus is distinguishing him from the gospel Jesus, which was shaped through the Pauline letters and centuries of the institutional churches' doctrines. Do the gospels provide any clues to uncover the historical Jesus?

After Paul's dramatic conversion, did the disciples share Jesus' original message with him before sending him to the Greek synagogues? And if they did, how can we know whether Paul adhered to what he was told? The disputes in Corinth and Galatia suggest that even in the earliest decades, competing interpretations of Jesus' message were already emerging.

One of the issues in dealing with the historical Jesus belongs to the message he preached throughout Israel. If we use John the baptizer as a barometer he could have been preaching about the return to the law, a need evidenced by the presence of the Romans. If we take the cursed fig tree, as I argued in Chapter 1, as a symbol of Israel's spiritual condition, then Jesus' message may have carried a religious edge: a critique of a priesthood that was out of season, without fruit, or failing in its vocation under Roman rule. If we take his charge to the Pharisees and Herodians about giving to God what is God's then we see a political message.

So, who was the historical Jesus? On the surface, all we know about him comes from the four Gospels which are consistent with his name, that he had at least three close disciples, that he traveled across what we call the Holy Land, and was crucified in Jerusalem. Beyond that, there are references to his disciples in Paul's letters and the Acts of the Apostles.

Initially, I believed he bore similarities to John the Baptist, whose message centered on change and release from the burden of sins. Elijah and the other prophets are particularly significant in illustrating this idea.

During times of crisis, whether Israel's exile to Babylon, occupation by the Seleucid Empire, famine, or other perils, the prophets called for a return to the law, believing it could save the people from their plight. In that sense, John's preaching fits the prophetic pattern: a call to return in the face of crisis, even though the restoration of Israel as a nation would not occur until nearly nineteen centuries later, in 1948.

I believe that while Jesus was traveling throughout Israel, he heard about the Roman prefect raiding the temple treasury to fund an aqueduct, an act that sparked a revolt in 26 CE (Josephus *Antiquities* 18.3.2 and 18.60–62), shortly prior to Pilate's arrival. It is easy to imagine him feeling compelled to return to Jerusalem to confront the Romans over this theft. A statement preserved in the synoptic Gospels may reflect the message he intended for Pilate: "Render to Caesar the things that are Caesar's, and to God the things that are God's" (Mark 12:17; Matt 22:21; Luke 20:25). He spoke these words in the presence of the Herodians, a group aligned more with Rome than with Judah, and it is easy to imagine them carrying such a statement back to Pilate. In effect, he was accusing Rome of stealing from God. Pilate would not have dismissed his words as they would indicate that he was aligning himself, even indirectly, with the growing movement of insurrection. The temple treasury was built from the offerings of ordinary people, including people like the widow who gave her mite. It embodied the faith and sacrifices of the community. Its violation was not only sacrilege but a profound betrayal of those who worshipped there—a betrayal so deep that it helped ignite a rebellion lasting about ten years.

If we consider Barabbas as a symbolic representation of Jesus as the "Son of the Father," it opens a window into understanding the historical Jesus. Barabbas is described as a murderer during an insurrection (Mark 15:7) and a participant in rebellion in the city

(Luke 23:19), both descriptions present him as a figure linked to social and political unrest, which may connect to the Jewish revolt and the timeframe surrounding Jesus' death. Such a connection raises the possibility that someone by the name of Jesus was viewed as a hero by the Jewish people. The gospels are in agreement that Jesus was crucified, a Roman practice that was typically reserved for those involved in acts of insurrection and other serious crimes like murder.

Looking closely at the events surrounding Pilate's interrogation of Jesus, the courtyard scene, and Jesus being led away to be scourged, we can glean further insights into the historical Jesus. The gospel narrative is framed by two moments: Jesus being taken away from Pilate and later being led away to be scourged and executed. Between these two scenes stands the release of a man involved in the insurrection in the city—Barabbas. The interrogation of Jesus by the priests prior to Pilate's questioning raises an important question: Why would the priests incite the crowd to demand the release of an insurrectionist while calling for the execution of the king of the Jews, unless it was to protect someone who spoke up for them? Their anger over Pilate's use of the temple treasury for the aqueduct may provide the answer. It positions the historical Jesus as a figure of reverence and even heroism for the priests; someone who confronted Roman sacrilege when Rome stole from God. After his arrest, Pilate confronts Jesus as a political rival and a potential king of the Jews. Jesus rejects the accusation with the words, "You say it," or as I argued earlier, "you say it for yourself."

As I explained in chapter 3, Barabbas symbolized those entering baptism and the church, indebted to the historical Jesus whose crucifixion gave them release.

In light of this, we can also consider how those closest to Jesus understood him. Before Jesus went toJerusalem, he preached a message outside the walled city that drew many who were eager to hear his words. How did his disciples and the multitudes who followed him react to his death? His execution did not end in their despair. His message had clearly taken root among his followers; they experienced a deeper understanding of his life and purpose.

In the wake of his death, they did not abandon his vision. They embraced it with greater resolve, believing he had given his life for them. Jesus came to embody the very hope the Gospels say he proclaimed, the goal toward which their own lives were now directed.

WHAT DO WE DO WITH THE GOSPEL JESUS?

I begin by stating that I am a Christian, not a Judeo-Christian. My faith is shaped by the Christian scriptures rather than the Old and New Testaments. My Christ is the Gospel Jesus, whose historical existence is less important to me than the story of his life and teachings, which guide how I strive to live.

Allow me to explain. In the United States, many call our country Christian, likely because most of the population professes some form of the religion. Yet I believe that denominations or individual churches cannot be Christian; only individuals can be—according to what I read in the Gospels and in Paul's authentic letters. We are not born into the faith, nor do rituals make us Christian. The rituals we practice are declarations of our intention to take up the mantle of Christ and follow.

So how do I live with the name Christian when what I have just written about the historical Jesus seems to stand in tension with the scriptures? Perhaps I am an optimist, but I believe in the ideal, that all who choose to change are included in God's realm. I believe the Jesus of the Gospels was a person of deep humanity, one who refused to let culture or position override the goodness he shared with the other. And I believe the Jesus of history and the Jesus of the Gospels lived and died for the benefit of others.

What can we glean about the historical Jesus from his disciples other than what Paul directly addressed or what Luke references in Acts? Surprisingly little, save perhaps the letter attributed to James, a text that may or may not have been written during Paul's lifetime. Outside of the Gospels and Acts, there are no surviving written accounts from James, John, or Peter that shed light on the historical Jesus.

LOVING OTHERS AS THE GOSPEL JESUS TAUGHT

Why do I believe in the gospel Jesus? In the United States, many people do not fit the cultural paradigms: those with weight issues, people of color, people who do not speak English, non-Christians, LGBTQ+ individuals, the unemployed, those in need or receiving government assistance, those with political differences, and many others. Too often these individuals are looked down upon with varying degrees of superiority and bigotry. Yet the gospel Jesus commanded us to love our neighbors without qualification (Mark 12:31), to love others as he loved us without qualification (John 13:34), and to do good for the least without qualification (Matt 25:40). He warned against judging others (Matt 7:1), for God alone judges through the Spirit. Paul affirmed that all are one in Christ, and the author of Ephesians proclaimed that Christ brings down the walls that divide us (2:14b). What this means is that being a member of a Christian denomination is not enough; we bring down those dividing walls only when we practice the compassion he embodied.

This world would be better if more people embraced the teachings of the gospel Jesus. Imagine a faith where being Christian did not require "joining up," or even being called a Christian. The only requirement would be to love God and neighbors without distinction. Paul's words in 1 Corinthians would ring true: "And if I have all faith, so as to remove mountains, but have not love, I am nothing" (13:2b). This love, expressed through compassion, kindness, and selflessness by those who take up the mantle of a Christ, could break down barriers and heal divisions across communities.

THE GOSPEL JESUS IN MARK

Who is the gospel Jesus in Mark? In my reading, he stands alongside figures like the Greek Prometheus, who preserved humankind from destruction; the Roman Aeneas, who followed the gods' will to found an eternal city; and Paul, who carried his message from Jerusalem to Illyricum and Rome. The teaching of Mark's Jesus aligns far more closely with the theology of Paul than with that of John the baptizer, the disciples James and John, Moses, or Elijah. Essentially, this Jesus is a combination of mythic heroes, Paul and a man caught up in an insurrection.

A NOTE ON PAUL'S DEATH

After much thought, I have come to believe that the account by Suetonius, who wrote that Christians caused a disturbance in Rome because of the execution of "Chrestus" in 64 CE (*Divus Claudius* 25.4) may actually refer to Paul's death. The riot occurred some thirty years after Jesus' execution in Jerusalem but much closer in time to Paul's. A Christian community already existed in Rome long before Paul sent them his letter from Illyricum; they would have known of Jesus' death well before his arrival. We have no evidence that the historical Jesus was ever called "Chrestus" until after Paul's letters circulated through his evangelism of Greece. Luke places the title "the Christ" on Peter's lips in Acts, a work written after his gospel and after Paul's death.

A RECENT MARTYR OF SORTS

While editing this manuscript, I heard an Episcopal bishop invoke the gospel's message in addressing the President of the United States, urging compassion toward vulnerable people. Throughout history, the teachings of Jesus, Paul, and others shaped by the Christian scriptures have carried similar messages to leaders of nations. Yet these teachings did not simply encourage mercy; they demanded it. In both Jesus' and Paul's cases, their uncompromising call for justice and compassion ultimately led to their executions.

HOW IT ALL STARTED

Jesus and his three disciples traveled through the countryside outside Jerusalem preaching that their religious institution had become corrupt. Encouraged by the response, he and his followers took that message to the temple. There he charged the priests with turning the people's house of worship into a commercial venture for their own gain. The priests were angered and decided to hunt down those who followed him and bring them back to Jerusalem for punishment.

After the incident, the Roman prefect took money from the temple treasury, which led to an insurrection. When Jesus heard of the defilement of the temple, he returned to Jerusalem and either took part in the uprising or confronted the Romans or Herodians, insisting that the temple's money belonged to God, not Rome. In doing so, he was judged to be an enemy of Rome and executed.

The disciples continued to preach his message, and the priests hired Paul to track them down. After bringing some members of the Way to Jerusalem, he witnessed Stephen's defense and stoning. On the road to Damascus to retrieve more followers, he had a moment of regret, realizing that Stephen's words made sense. He then approached members of the Way, joined them, and began preaching their message in the synagogues of Judea.

Because Paul was from Tarsus, part of the Greek world, the disciples asked him to take the message to the synagogues there. His first attempts were met with rejection, and he was even imprisoned.

In Lystra, a district of Galatia, something happened and the message changed. My claim is that he met Philemon, a wealthy and literate man familiar with Greek and Roman history and drama. I believe he provided housing for Paul and persuaded him to see another way to shape his theology. Paul responded, began welcoming Gentiles, and formed a church there. When the disciples learned he was not requiring circumcision or observance of the law, they confronted him. I came to the conclusion that Paul changed the message because of Philemon and the response he was receiving.

Paul's theology developed to the point that all people, regardless of nationality, social status, or sex, could enter the kingdom of God through Jesus Christ, something he said came to him in a vision.

After forming several churches, Paul traveled to Dalmatia, where he wrote his letter to the Romans, likely with Philemon's help. He then journeyed to Rome, refused to call Nero lord, saying he had only one Lord, Jesus Christ, and was executed. His death sparked a riot among the Christians, as Suetonius reported.

I believe Philemon then wrote Mark, using the historical Jesus and Paul's theology of inclusion to give the fledgling movement a foundation. He appealed to the Greeks through *Prometheus Bound*, philosophy, and imagery they recognized, and to the Romans through the *Aeneid* and the centurion at the cross.

Epilogue

"Whoever, therefore, thinks that he understands the divine scriptures, or any part of them, so that it does not build up the love of God and neighbor, does not understand it at all."

—Augustine

I began my study hoping to show that my liberal philosophy was rooted in the gospel rather than the other way around. After more than thirty years of study and reflection, I have concluded that being a Christian is something being practiced, a way of living that will lead to a better life for all. I believe that aligns with the Jesus found in the Gospel of Mark and with Paul who welcomed Gentiles into his communities with only the necessities of faith and compassion.

There is a song *If I Can Dream* that prays for a better land that offers a place where we can live together in peace, a sentiment that echoes Paul's hope that there is neither Jew nor Greek and Mark's accounts of Jesus welcoming the untouchables into his kingdom. I am a Christian, and I believe in that ideal—the one I see at the heart of Christianity in its beginning. Unfortunately, our world of tradition and culture prevent that from becoming a reality.

Before closing, I want to address a question that has followed me throughout this work.

WHY PUBLISH THE MANUSCRIPT?

Why would I choose to have my manuscript published? This question has followed me throughout my study. What I have uncovered has the potential to unsettle the faith of millions and give the Mythists information for their arguments.

I once asked a single mother of two how she might feel if she learned that the historical Jesus and the gospel Jesus were not the same person. Her response was poignant: she said she would rather not know. A lawyer I spoke with asked a similar question—why publish it at all, knowing it could disturb deeply held beliefs?

I thought of these conversations when I read the novel and watched the televised film *The Word*, in which a newly discovered gospel, allegedly written by James the brother of Jesus, turns out to be a forgery. The public relations man promoting it faced a moral dilemma: reveal the truth and shatter people's hopes, or keep silent. A similar tension appears in *The Da Vinci Code*, where the protagonist must decide whether to conceal or reveal the identity of a supposed descendant of Jesus and Mary Magdalene.

So why publish my manuscript? I am still a Christian because I believe in the language of Ephesians, that Christ brings all the dividing walls down and that when we help each other we are in the will of God. Why would God prefer those who have much to those who have little or nothing? If there is a God like that, I want no part of it. My wife and I have a truism: "We are in this together, and no one gets out alive."

Even so, I have no quarrel with anyone practicing the religion of their choice, so long as they grant me the same freedom. What I have discovered in my study is something I believe: all people deserve access to their beliefs. Everyone should have the opportunity to weigh and process this information for themselves, just as I have had to do.

A public figure recently said, "Pick up a Bible off your shelf and read it. That's my worldview." His statement needs a clarifier: which part of the Bible, and who decides how it should be read. In my view, no one holds that authority for anyone else. Each of us must wrestle with the text ourselves, guided by conscience and by the compassion at the heart of the gospel Jesus taught.

Bibliography

Aeschylus. *Prometheus Bound and Other Plays*. Translated by Philip Vellacott. Penguin Classics, 2001.

Burckhardt, Jacob. *History of Greek Culture*. American Book Company, 1888.

Cavendish, Richard, ed. *Mythology: An Illustrated Encyclopedia of the Principal Myths and Religions of the World*. Orbis, 1980.

The Holy Bible: Revised Standard Version. Harper Study Bible and Oxford Annotated Bible. Zondervan, 1971.

Josephus. *Against Apion*. Translated by H. St. J. Thackeray. Loeb Classical Library. Harvard University Press, 1926.

———. *Jewish Antiquities*. Translated by H. St. J. Thackeray et al. Loeb Classical Library. Harvard University Press, 1930–65.

———. *The Jewish War*. Translated by H. St. J. Thackeray. Loeb Classical Library. Harvard University Press, 1927.

Lactantius. *On the Deaths of the Persecutors*. Translated by J. L. Creed. Oxford Early Christian Texts. Oxford University Press, 1984.

Liddell, Henry George, and Robert Scott. *A Greek–English Lexicon*. American Book Company, 1888.

Philo. *On the Embassy to Gaius*. Translated by F. H. Colson. Loeb Classical Library. Harvard University Press, 1940.

Schmidt, Michael. *The First Poets: Lives of the Ancient Greek Poets*. Knopf, 2004.

Suetonius. *The Twelve Caesars*. Translated by Robert Graves, revised by J. B. Rives. Penguin Classics. Penguin Books, 2007.

United Bible Societies. *Greek New Testament: A Reader's Edition*. Deutsche Bibelgesellschaft, 2007.

Virgil. *The Aeneid*. Translated by Robert Fitzgerald. Vintage Classics, 1990.

www.ingramcontent.com/pod-product-compliance
Lightning Source LLC
LaVergne TN
LVHW020652100826
845148LV00012B/2451